CANADA at the OLYMPICS

THE FIRST HUNDRED YEARS

1896 - 1996

CANADA at the OLYMPICS

THE FIRST HUNDRED YEARS

infact

EDITED BY JACK BATTEN

ISBN: 1-8960-9203-9

INFACT Publishing
66 Portland St.
2nd Floor
Toronto, ON
M5V 2M8

INFACT Publishing is an official licensee of the Canadian Olympic Association.

Jacket and text design: Andrew Smith
Page composition: Andrew Smith Graphics Inc.

Project Editor: Anne Holloway
Photo Research: Dolores Gubasta/KLIX The Picture Network

Printed and bound in Canada by Metropole Litho

CONTENTS

FOREWORD

For now, because he's fresh in our minds, let's take Donovan Bailey as a handy symbol of Canadian achievement in a century of Olympic Games. There he was, on the second Saturday night of the 1996 Games in Atlanta, just after he crossed the finish line in the 100-metre race, his face exploding in an unforgettable expression compounded of triumph, amazement and euphoria. Triumph that he had beaten the fastest group of runners ever to compete in the event. Amazement that he had broken the world record. And euphoria that he was taking home a gold medal. It was a moment for Bailey, for all of us, Canadians, to savour, to remember with elation and pride.

But, as *Canada at the Olympics: The First Hundred Years* makes clear in words and pictures, Bailey isn't the only athlete, nor his run the only victory, that deserves such a hallowed place in our Olympic history. Over the 100 years of the Games, both Summer and Winter, Canada's men and women have stirred the nation with magnificent performances. Billy Sherring in the 1906 marathon. Barbara Ann Scott in the 1948 figure skating. Kerrin-Lee Gartner in the 1992 downhill skiing. Like Bailey, each won gold. Like Bailey, each has a story that deserves to be told and retold. And there are many more. Double gold medallist Percy Williams in the 100- and 200-metre sprints in 1928. Sylvie Fréchette in the 1992 synchronized swimming. Gold and stories. And, yes, there has been heartbreak for Canadians in the Games—the times when Canadians faltered just for a moment—and that, too, finds its place in the book.

In a sense, this is a book of Olympic moments, framed in the text, caught in the photographs. All kinds of moments, but especially the ones that smack of greatness. Donovan Bailey's may be the freshest in our minds, but *Canada at the Olympics: The First Hundred Years* brings all of them, all of the earlier victories and the stories behind them, back to glorious life.

CHAPTER ONE

DAWN of the MODERN GAMES

THE GAMES OF 1896-1912

JAMES A. BARCLAY

THE LONGEST-RUNNING SHOW ON EARTH, THE OLYMPIC GAMES OF ANCIENT Greece, emerged from the mists of antiquity to recorded history in 776 B.C. These Games came to be held every four years, one of several sporting festivals dedicated to ancient gods, in this case Zeus. The poet Homer had located heaven at the top of Mount Olympus, the highest peak in Greece, and a logical home for the god who controlled the skies, so the sporting contests dedicated to Zeus came to be known as the Olympic Games.

The oldest Olympic event was the *stade*, a race the length of the stadium, or about 200 metres. Other events were added over the years; these included the pentathlon (a five-discipline competition consisting of running, jumping, javelin, discus, and wrestling), boxing, chariot racing, and horseback riding.

Since the ancient Greek Games, wrestling has been a popular Olympic sport. Today's Olympic wrestlers compete in 20 events.

The contestants who came to Olympia from the city states of Greece conferred on it not only status and political prestige but also wealth, just as the modern Olympics supposedly do for host cities today. They often competed nude, a custom discreetly ignored by the Victorians who revived the Olympics, as was the other ancient custom of animal and human sacrifices.

The Greek Games came to an end in A.D. 394 when the Romans, who controlled Greece at the time, abolished them.

These ancient games played an important role in the physical education of the Greeks, a fact that was not lost on the man who resurrected the Olympics in 1896, Baron Pierre de Coubertin. Born into an aristocratic family, the diminutive Coubertin was a scholar and an educator whose mission was the revival of the Olympic Games. Coubertin believed in the moral influence of physical culture: that the international prowess of countries like

Baron Pierre de Coubertin, the founder of the modern Olympic movement, believed in the moral improvement of young men, and of nations, through sport.

Britain and Germany flowed from their insistence on giving youth a fine physical education; that if nations met more often on the field of sport, they would meet less often in battle.

The British, Swedes, and Greeks had tried to revive the Olympics earlier in the nineteenth century. But it was Coubertin, by dint of persuasion and subterfuge, who finally succeeded in launching a larger and more permanent Olympic movement.

His starting point was a meeting at the Sorbonne in 1894 that brought together international delegates at a sports conference. The delegates found themselves authorizing the 31-year-old Coubertin to form an International Olympic Committee and to plan the first of the modern Olympics for Athens. The plan was that the IOC would be made up not of representatives of countries but rather of sports associations in these countries. The Olympiad — a word now synonymous with Olympic Games but originally meaning the interval between the Games — was set at four years.

In 1896, there were few national sports organizations in the world, so spreading the word about this new idealistic international venture proved difficult. Nevertheless, some 311 competitors, all male, from 30 nations — Canada wasn't one of them — turned up for the first modern Olympic Games held before 40,000 spectators under the royal patronage of the King of Greece.

In 1896, Athens fittingly became the site of the first modern Olympics, in which 311 athletes from 30 countries competed. Canada did not send its first official Olympic team until 1908.

As a condition of the Second Olympics being held in Paris in 1900, Coubertin had to agree to staging it as part of the Exposition Universelle already planned for the city. As a result, the Games lost their identity. Indeed, the word Olympic did not appear on any program, and the events were spread over two months.

The individual events made a curious hodge-podge: cricket, lawn tennis, rugby, golf, baseball, polo, pelota, angling, automobilism, bowling, running wild-boar shooting, live and clay pigeon shooting, blind man's bluff, fire-fighting, three-legged racing, leap-frog, tug-of-war, cannon-shooting, and skating (the skaters found themselves listed as participants in the cutlery exhibition). It's not clear whether all these events, though listed, actually took place, and it was only after the Games that the IOC decided which events were official.

The Montreal Amateur Athletic Association was the most active sports organization in 19th-century Canada. Pictured above is the MAAA Gymnasium Group.

Although a few Canadians competed individually in 1900, 1904, and 1906, Canada did not select and send a team to the Olympics until 1908.

Ice skating was an Olympic event in the Fourth Olympiad of 1908, but otherwise the Games before the First World War were confined to summer sports, most of which had taken early root in Canada. Montreal was the mother city of athletics in Canada. Back in 1842, Montrealers had formed an Olympic Club for foot racing and other summer sports. It organized the Athletic Games, later changing the name to Olympic Games. The Montreal Amateur Athletic Association (MAAA) was incorporated in 1881 and held its first track meet in the same year.

In 1883 the MAAA helped form the Amateur Athletic Association of Canada (AAA of C) as a safeguard against a growing professionalism in baseball, sculling, foot-racing, and in Canada's national sport, lacrosse. In the following year the AAA of C held its first annual track and field championships on the grounds of the Montreal Lacrosse Club. For a number of years these championships were held in alternate years in Montreal and Toronto. The AAA of C was renamed the Canadian Amateur Athletic Association (CAAA) in 1898, and in 1909 the MAAA and the CAAA formed the Amateur Athletic Union of Canada (AAU of C), which controlled amateur sport in Canada for some 50 years.

In 1898, the Canadian Intercollegiate Athletic Union was formed, followed two years later by the Ontario Amateur Athletic Association, the first association in Canada formed solely for track and field. The Hamilton Amateur Athletic Club had been organized along the lines of the MAAA and quickly became the leading track and field club in Canada. The Maritimes had their own amateur athletic association by 1888.

Canadians competed internationally long before a Canadian team was sent to the Olympics. A crew from Saint John, New Brunswick, had taken first prize at a regatta in Paris. Toronto's Argonaut Rowing Club, founded in 1872, was soon winning at American regattas. An Argo crew won the World's Fair Regatta on Lake Geneva. The storied tug-of-war team from Zorra, Ontario, pulled

The Zorra, Ont., tug-of-war team was victorious at the Chicago World's Fair. Tug-of-war was listed as an Olympic event in the 1900 Paris Olympics.

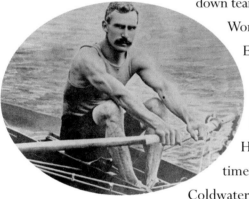

down teams from five other countries at the Chicago World's Fair. A Canadian lacrosse team visited England and played before Queen Victoria. Canadian professional scullers Ned Hanlan and Jake Gaudaur won races in the United States and Britain, and Canadian sprinter Harry Bethune was clocked at world-record time in San Francisco. George Gray of Coldwater, Ontario, won the American shotput title 10 times in the 1880s and 1890s. In 1900, Canada's Harry Gill won the all-round athletic event at the American Amateur Athletic championships, and Canadians came in first, second, and third in the Boston Marathon, with Hamilton's Jack Caffery, winner in 1900, repeating in 1901.

Given this interest and proficiency in sport, why did Canadians show so little interest in the first four modern Olympiads? The main reason was financial. Competitors had to pay their own way, and Canada's finest amateur athletes were middle or working class and could not afford it.

Jake Gaudaur (left above) and Ned Hanlan won several international rowing competitions. Hanlan, the first Canadian to win a world championship in any sport, was a six-time world champion until he was unseated in 1884.

At least two Canadians competed in the Second Olympiad in Paris in 1900, but as members of the U.S. team. George Orton of the University of Pennsylvania won the 3,000-metre steeplechase, and on the same day came third in the 400-metre hurdles. While at the University of Toronto, Orton had dominated middle-distance running in Canada and had raced internationally for the Toronto Lacrosse Club, winning a slew of Canadian titles, the U.S. mile title in 1892, and the English two-mile steeple-chase in 1898. After graduating from U of T, he attended the University of Pennsylvania and captained its track and field team. Orton has the distinction of being the first Canadian to win an Olympic gold medal.

Another member of the U.S. team was Canadian Ronald MacDonald. Born in Antigonish County, Nova Scotia, he attended Boston College. MacDonald won the Boston Marathon in 1898 and was doing well in 1899 until a roadside spectator handed him a sponge. (Was it soaked in chloroform, as MacDonald and his doctor later alleged ?) He ran in the Olympic Marathon in Paris and was the last of only seven to finish. Again, mystery surrounded this race. The French took the first three places, but rumour had it that they had taken shortcuts through the streets of Paris. Many years later MacDonald claimed that he and an American, who came sixth, were the only two to run the entire course.

Coubertin had hoped that the Third Olympiad of 1904, originally scheduled for Chicago, would restore the image of the Olympics. But James Sullivan, secretary of the American Amateur Athletic Association, and no friend of Coubertin, successfully supported a rival bid from St. Louis, which was hosting a world's fair and wanted to add the Olympic Games. As a result the Third Olympiad dragged on from May to November, becoming just a sideshow to the fair. Only 12 nations competed, and all but a few Europeans stayed away. Coubertin himself did not attend. Of the 554 competitors, 432 were American. Of the 74 medals in track and field, all but four went to Americans.

A few Canadians went to St. Louis under their own steam or with assistance from their clubs. They did well, coming away with four gold, one silver, and one bronze. Étienne Desmarteau of the Montreal Police Athletic Association (MPAA) threw the 56-pound weight further than any other man at St. Louis and prevented a clean sweep of the field events by Americans. This modest six-foot one-inch, 220-pound police-man had been throwing weights and discus for years and had earlier set a world record for a 56-pound throw. The MPAA had refused to sponsor his trip to St. Louis, and the Montreal Police had fired him for taking the time off. But the MAAA sponsored him, and when he returned to Montreal he found himself not only a hero but a reinstated policeman. Tragically, the 32-year-old Desmarteau died of typhoid a year later. His was the first individual Olympic gold medal credited to Canada.

The Galt Football Club from Ontario overwhelmed two U.S. teams, scored 11 goals to nil, and won the gold medal in soccer. The Galt team was financed by its own previous successes, money collected from spectators at events like the Chicago World's Fair, and during a tour of Manitoba in 1903, where it was unbeaten in 17 games.

Lacrosse was still Canada's national sport in 1904, and the Shamrock Lacrosse Club of Winnipeg won the first team gold medal of the 1904 Games for Canada.

Canada's fourth gold was probably the most dramatic. The 46-year-old George S. Lyon of Toronto's Lambton Golf Club was the only foreign entry in a field of 76 Americans who competed for the Olympic golf title at St. Louis. This grand old man of Canadian golf had taken up the game at the age of 37 after a lifetime of other sports,

The Shamrock Lacrosse Club of Winnipeg won the first team gold of the 1904 Games. Bronze was taken by the Mohawk Indians, a team from the Six Nations reserve near Brantford, Ont.

notably baseball, lacrosse, cricket (where he held the world record for the highest score in an innings), pole-vaulting (he is said to have held the Canadian record in the 1870s), and tennis. Having golfed for only three years, he proceeded to win the Canadian Amateur championship in 1898, and again in 1900 and 1903. But the Americans did not give him a ghost of a chance against their young champions, even less so when they witnessed what their press described as his "coal-heaver's swing." But in round after round of match play, Lyon mowed them down with his long hitting and steady nerves. In the final, played in a pitiless cold rain, Lyon convincingly beat a man half his age. He then proceeded to walk on his hands the full length of the clubhouse. Lyon went on to win more Canadian amateur golf championships than any man before or since.

Toronto's George S. Lyon swung his way to gold at St. Louis, beating 76 competing American golfers.

In 1906, the first and last Intercalated Games (held between Olympics) took place in Athens. Twenty nations sent 887 athletes. The IOC was behind the 1906 games, awarded Olympic medals, but did not consider the games as a full, numbered Olympiad. Canada won a gold and a silver, which is a better result than it might sound, for only four Canadian athletes made the long trip to Athens.

Don Linden of Toronto's West-End YMCA Athletic Club took silver in the 1,500-metre walk, but by all accounts should have taken gold: two of the four judges disqualified the American winner for improper footwork. Linden did not protest, but agreed to a walk-off with the alleged winner on the following day. The American did not turn up. The judges, influenced by Greece's King George, let the result stand.

Canada's top pole-vaulter, Ed Archibald, had the misfortune to lose his pole in Italy and went unplaced in competition. Elwood Hughes of Toronto injured himself in practice and had to drop out of the five-mile run and the marathon.

The final track and field event of the Olympics, the marathon, was for many years the glamour event of the Games. To win the Olympic marathon when it is run on the original course from Marathon to Athens must be the ultimate in track and field, even to this day. That was the accomplishment of Billy Sherring of Canada in 1906, and his thrilling win did much to spur future athletics in Canada.

The 1908 Games were scheduled for Rome, but in 1906 Mount Vesuvius erupted, the Italian economy suffered, and so the Fourth Olympiad was switched to London. The Irish objected to parading under the British flag, the Finns to parading under the Russian. The British reportedly could not find a U.S. flag to fly above the stadium, whereupon the U.S. flag-bearer in the march-past did not dip the flag as the team passed the Royal box. The American manager objected to being banned from the field by British officials. Most countries objected to all the officials being British. The Americans protested when they found no hole for the pole in the pole-vault, and no landing pit. (The Americans had a point. A hole had been allowed in 1906. Other vaulters used a pole with a spike.) When the Americans started digging a hole and a pit, Billy Sherring, now trainer to the Canadian team, protested. Canada's team complained about British food, our cyclists about the stadium track being too steeply banked. The Americans scorned the British regulation of knee-length running shorts and wore theirs mid-thigh. In retaliation for the blocking of their runner in the 400-metre final, the British officials cried foul and removed the finishing tape as an American was about to win. The Americans objected to a blind draw for the heats, since competitors from the same nation could be drawn against each other.

In 1908 Canada sent, for the first time, an official Olympic team, funded mainly by government: two dozen track and field athletes, plus sharpshooters, scullers, cyclists, and lacrosse players. This all-male team was selected by a Central Olympic Committee appointed in 1907. (Two years later it became the Canadian Olympic Association, a member of the AAU of C until 1949, when it became independent.) A few other Canadians received private sponsorship.

Canada came away with three gold, three silver, and nine bronze medals. The highlight was provided by Bobby Kerr's victory in the 200-metre dash, following a third for Kerr in the 100 metres. Just two weeks before the Olympics, the feisty Kerr, from Hamilton, Ontario, the same city that produced Billy Sherring, had won both the 100 and 220 yards in the British Championships, making him a joint favourite for the Olympics with the U.S. sprinter James Rector. But a South African runner came from out of nowhere in the 100 metres to whip both Kerr and Rector. Three judges awarded second place to Kerr, one judge favoured Rector, and when the referee sided with the single judge, it was Rector who got the silver, Kerr the bronze. Kerr was the only runner to compete in both the 100 and 200 metres, and, in the latter race, he edged out two Americans by less than a foot.

Canada's marksman Walter Ewing won the gold and George Beattie took the silver in trap-shooting, and both men were part of the Canadian team that came second in the trap-shooting team event. Ewing was then 30 and well-known in Montreal's business community. He had won the Clarendon Cup for shooting in 1906, but was virtually unknown in Britain, where he had to adapt to the British method of releasing the clay "bird" from the trap.

Our third gold went to the All Canadas lacrosse team, which defeated the British (the only other team in the event) by 14 to 10. The team was truly representative, with players from eight cities across Canada.

Bobby Kerr was a dual medal winner at the 1908 London Games, winning gold in the 200 m dash and bronze in the 100 m.

This page from the London Illustrated News shows the top finishers in the 1908 Olympic marathon. Like Canada's highly rated entrant, Tom Longboat, Britain's Dorando Pietri (centre) collapsed during the race, both probably owing to drug overdoses.

18

COG-WA-GEE
LONGBOAT

Canada's biggest disappointment was the defeat of Tom Longboat in the marathon. This Onondaga Indian runner from the Six Nations reserve near Brantford, Ontario, had set a record when he won the Boston Marathon in 1907. Longboat had been nearly disqualified for professionalism at least twice, and the Americans protested his appearance in the London Olympics. As a result, the Longboat saga occupied more space in Canadian newspapers than any other event.

Some 13 Canadians started in the marathon. At the 20-mile mark, when leading, Tom Longboat was stricken with a sudden weakness. He spun around and dropped on to the track, out of the race for good. He signed a professional contract a few months later and went on to win the World's Professional Marathon Championship, dubbed "The Race of the Century," in 1909.

Also disappointing was the failure of Canada's top sculler, Lou Scholes, to get any medal, and the Argos' eights and pairs for having to settle for bronze.

By 1912, Olympic fever had begun to take hold. While 23 nations had sent just over 2,000 competitors, including 36 women, to London, 29 nations sent 2,447 competitors, including 57 women, to the Fifth Olympiad at Stockholm.

Tom Longboat (previous page), a Six Nations Indian distance runner, broke numerous records during his career, but failed to finish the 1908 Olympic marathon. During World War I, Longboat put his talent to patriotic use as a dispatch runner in France.

Opening Ceremonies of the 1912 Stockholm Olympics.

Before the First World War a few Olympic events were held for women in archery, tennis, and golf. Figure skating was added in 1908, aquatics in 1912. No Canadian women competed in these events. Still labouring under the Victorian delusion that women were too fragile for sports, the IOC did not schedule women's track and field events until 1928.

In Stockholm there was a return to the international good fellowship and harmony that Coubertin had envisaged. Reported one Canadian newspaper: "The Canadians, Americans and English are training together in the most friendly way." King Gustav of Sweden, as patron, attended the spectacular Opening Ceremonies. Some innovations that made an appearance at Stockholm were a new stadium equipped with a public address system and electronic timing devices (races could now be timed to one-tenth of a second), and running lanes delineated by chalk instead of cord tied to pickets.

Canada's team numbered only half that sent to London and won half as many medals. Canadian swimmer George Hodgson won two gold medals and broke several world records. This slightly built 18-year-old McGill University student belonged to a well-known Montreal family, many of whose members excelled at sports. A year

George Hodgson was Canada's first Olympic swimming champion, setting freestyle records that remained unbroken from 1912 to 1924.

George Goulding strode to gold in the 10,000 m walk at Stockholm; he later won 300 invitational races in Canada, the U.S., Britain.

Vancouver policeman Duncan Gillis was a silver medallist in the hammer throw at Stockholm.

earlier, Hodgson had won the one-mile freestyle at the Festival of Empire Sports in London. In the heats of the 1,500-metre freestyle at Stockholm, he twice broke a world record before setting a new record in the final, which he won by the clear margin of 39 seconds. On the way, he broke the 1,000-metre world record and he continued swimming to break the record for the mile. Four days later Hodgson won gold again in the 400-metre freestyle after breaking the world record in the semi-finals.

Canada's other gold medal went to George Goulding of Toronto's YMCA in the 10-kilometre walk. Goulding had competed in 1908 as both a walker and a runner, but had been unplaced. In Stockholm the news that his first-born was a boy and that Mrs. Goulding was doing well reportedly had him "going great guns." Goulding faced nine other competitors in the final of the walking race, set the pace from the start, eager to establish a new world record, and only the 40-year-old Ernest Webb of Britain made a race of it. Goulding was some 30 metres ahead with 1,500 to go and increased his lead to nearly 80 metres with only a lap remaining. He won easily, with Webb second, but he failed to beat Webb's world record.

Among other Canadian medallists, Vancouver policeman Duncan Gillis took silver in the 16-pound hammer throw, and Saskatchewan-born dentist Cal Bricker came second in the long jump. Toronto Argonaut sculler Everard Butler won bronze in the single sculls; William Happeny of Montreal tied for third in the pole-vault; and Frank Lukeman tied for bronze in the pentathlon.

In 1914, Coubertin designed the flag of the interlocked Olympic rings, representing the five continents of the Olympics' contestants, but it was not to fly for six years. The Sixth Olympiad had been scheduled for Berlin in 1916. When war broke out in 1914, the Canadian delegate to the IOC, James Merrick, was confident that the Games would be held. "The war is not likely to last for four months," he blithely forecast. Later that year there was talk of switching the Games to Stockholm, and later still to the United States. By year's end some organizers were conceding that the 1916 Games might not take place at all. And so it proved: for four years the world had more pressing matters on its mind.

Long jumper Cal Bricker was a two-time Olympic medallist, bringing home bronze in 1908, and silver in 1912 with a jump of 7.21 m.

Profile

Billy Sherring

Gold Medallist, Marathon, 1906

Billy Sherring was 29 when he won the Olympic marathon in 1906. He had been a leading long-distance runner with the Hamilton YMCA for seven years, winner of the *Hamilton Herald* Road Race, second in the Boston Marathon, and the Canadian 10-mile record holder. To pay his way to Athens he had to rely on raising money from friends and admirers. He gave up his job and left for Greece on a cattle-boat two months before his race. In Athens, he found a job as a railway station porter. He wrote home complaining about having to pay "$2.40 a day for board and extra for baths and light." But he maintained his usual cocky optimism: "The fellow that beats me will be a dandy."

Hamilton's Billy Sherring crosses the marathon finish line accompanied by the Crown Prince of Greece at the 1906 Intercalated Games, held in Athens to commemorate the tenth anniversary of the first modern Games.

Sherring was by now an experienced and shrewd marathoner. He had been leading the Boston Marathon in 1900 but had paced himself poorly and finished second. Six years after his Olympic gold medal, he recalled his victory: "I managed to pull down one after another until at 10 miles I was up with the leader, Blake of Australia. I had trained with Blake and I knew that he was a speedy runner, but I was not sure if he could go the distance or not. After running with him until near the 15-mile mark, he suddenly gave up...and from there on I ran alone....After running about 19 miles, I decided to slow down to a walk. I walked for nearly two miles off and on, and then the crowd of people started to cheer me, and as I did not understand the language I took it for granted that someone was coming behind me and I started to run again. The thermometer was well over the 90° mark, and I was certainly glad when I learned that I had won." The Crown Prince of Greece ran the last few yards with Sherring as he crossed the finishing line.

The news of Sherring's win electrified not only the city of Hamilton where Billy had been born and bred, but the nation. It captured the headlines of Canada's newspapers, replacing the latest news of the San Francisco earthquake. The *Globe* waxed lyrical: "...from a country far past the Pillars of Hercules, beyond Atlantis or the wildest dreams of the most daring Phoenician navigators, came a young man who conquered the fleetest."

Hamilton's mayor initially opined that the city was too broke to afford a reception for the returning hero, but wiser heads prevailed. Sherring was feted in London, England; met by Hamiltonians when he landed at New York; wined and dined by Montrealers and Torontonians; given a torchlight procession and official reception in Hamilton; and finished up over $7,000 to the good. Wisely, he immediately gave up competitive running.

The *Hamilton Herald* Road Race is today known as the Billy Sherring Memorial Around The Bay Race.

CHAPTER TWO

A TASTE of GOLD

THE GAMES OF 1920-1928

FRANK COSENTINO

BARON PIERRE DE COUBERTIN'S NEW FIVE-RINGED OLYMPIC FLAG FLEW over the city of Antwerp, Belgium, from April 20 to September 12, 1920. The flag of every nation in the world was represented by at least one of the rings' colours; the white background symbolized peace, the hoped-for result of the "war to end all wars."

War and its devastation were still on everybody's mind. Europe remained in the process of recovering, nowhere more so than in tiny Belgium, whose cities had been levelled and whose people had suffered thousands of casualties. It was an inspiring symbol of optimism that youthful athletes were coming together to celebrate and compete — rather than fight — in such surroundings. The postwar revival of the Olympic Games, the first ones held since 1912, was as much about psychology as it was about international competition.

The Great War signalled a distinct end to the graceful Edwardian era. Gone were the old ways. This was the Jazz Age, a time of rising hemlines and rising expectations. Perhaps as a response to the new world order, Olympic officials decided to move in

The Winnipeg Falcons were Canada's first Olympic hockey team. Their gold medal victory in 1920 established Canada's pre-eminence in the sport, at which our teams remained unbeaten until 1936.

some new directions. For Canadians, a key change was the inclusion of ice hockey in the Games. It wasn't the first time that a winter sport had been incorporated in the Olympics program; figure skating appeared in the London Games of 1908. But this was *hockey*, a game that had made its way from Canada to Europe in the 1890s.

The Winnipeg Falcons provided Canada's representation at the 1920 Games. The Falcons won the right by whipping the University of Toronto for the Allan Cup, symbol of Canadian Senior hockey supremacy. Of the eight Falcons on the Olympic team, seven were of Icelandic extraction, six had fought in the war, and five had only recently returned to Canada. Now, in mid-April of 1920, they were on their way back to the very scene of the battles they had been lucky enough to survive.

When the Falcons reached Belgium, what they found waiting for them, apart from a royal reception from the grateful Belgians and from the British troops still stationed in the region, was a series of surprises. Olympic rules called for seven-man hockey played over two periods. That was old-fashioned hockey to the Canadians, who had long since converted to six men and three periods. The small Olympic ice surface, a mere 70 by 175 feet, presented problems, too.

But once the Falcons hit the ice, they brushed aside worries about rules and rink size. In the team's first game, against the newly created nation of Czechoslovakia, Canada ran up a 15−0 score. Haldor Halderson led the Canadians with seven goals, but the player who dazzled the spectators was the remarkably swift Mike Goodman, who was also the North American speed-skating champion. Some were convinced that his skates must have had wings attached. One spectator even offered him $100 for them! The game provided an amazing display. Canada did not incur a single penalty; it did not allow a single shot on goal.

Canada entered the second round. Its opponent this time was the United States, which had defeated the Swiss 29−0. Not only did Canada's traditional American rivals have a strong team, they also had the benefit of three transplanted Canadians and a huge contingent of American servicemen in the stands. Nevertheless, Canada won 2−0. Both goals came in the second period, one on what was described as a "corkscrew rush" by Frank Frederickson.

Canada's final opponent for the gold medal was Sweden, which had won its second game over France 4−0. The major surprise of the title game was not that Canada won, scoring 12 goals; it was that the Swedes actually scored one on the Canadians. Goalie Wally Byron was so surprised that he fell to the ice in shock. Regardless, Canada had won its first gold medal of the 1920 Games.

When the Opening Ceremonies of the 1920 Games took place on August 14, the new Belgian stadium, hastily erected, was filled with 30,000 spectators who heard Belgian fencer Victor Boin take the Olympic oath for the first time on behalf of all competitors. White doves of peace were set loose to fly across the stadium, announcing that nations had put aside their differences to compete without rancour. While there might have been a cessation in hostilities, bitter memories lingered. Germany and Austria were not invited to these Games.

Among the 3,000 athletes from 27 countries at the Games, 56 made up the Canadian team. They produced splendid results; the boxing team won five medals, including one gold; swimming star George Vernot of Montreal accounted for two medals, a bronze in the 400 metres and a silver in the 1,500 metres; and Earl Thomson came through with the gold in the 110-metre hurdles. But from the very start, Canada's performance was marked by curiosities. In the Opening Ceremonies, the Canadian delegation found itself without a flag. No Canadian Ensign was available. The solution? Canadian flag-bearer Archie McDiarmid marched in the procession carrying a bare flag-pole. If that seemed odd, so did the mix of national allegiances among some of Canada's gold-medal heroes.

The gold medal hurdler, Earl Thomson, a six-foot-three, 195-pound athlete, was more noted in the United States, where he was proficient in a variety of track and field events including low hurdles, high hurdles, shotput, broad jump, discus, hammer throw, javelin, pole-vault, and the 200 metres. Thomson was born in 1895 in Birch Hills near Prince Albert, Saskatchewan. When he was eight, the family moved to California where he played sport, won a scholarship to Dartmouth University and captained its track team. All the while, he retained his Canadian citizenship; he had even fought in the war with the RCAF. Although he had become the premier hurdler in the United States, his never having relinquished his Canadian citizenship made him ineligible to compete for his adopted country.

In spite of the heavy track at Antwerp, Thomson bested the 27 other competitors to win the 110-metre-hurdle gold in a world record time of 14.8 seconds. At the medal presentation ceremony, the Canadian Ensign was still not

Swimmer George Vernot stroked his way to two medals at the 1920 Games—a bronze in the 400 m and a silver in the 1,500 m freestyle.

available. Officials hastily borrowed an English flag, which they flew above the American standards for the silver and bronze medallists.

American-trained but Canadian-born hurdler Earl Thomson (far left) set a world record of 14.8 seconds to win a gold medal at Antwerp.

If Earl Thomson was a curiosity because of his Canadian birth and American training, Bert Schneider, gold medal winner in the welterweight boxing class, was even more unusual. Schneider was born in Cleveland, Ohio, and moved to Montreal when still an infant but retained his American citizenship. As an adult, he competed in such diverse sports as water polo and boxing. The Canadian Olympic Committee never thought to check his nationality; he was the Canadian welterweight champion, had been part of the Montreal scene for years, and was invited to the Olympic trials, which he won.

After receiving a bye in the first round, Schneider successfully fought the South African contestant to a unanimous decision. He knocked out Aage Steen, of Norway, to advance to the next round, the semi-finals, against Frederick Colberg of the United States. His victory over Colberg assured him of the gold medal match with Alex Ireland of Great Britain. The final was a standoff. At the end of the match, each boxer sat wearily in his corner. The referee declared it a draw; the new rules in place called for an extra round, overtime. At the end of this round, it was the superbly conditioned Schneider who was smiling: he had won a gold medal for Canada, his home but not so native land.

31

When the Winter Games convened in 1924 at Chamonix, France, they did so over the objections of the Scandinavians. Both Sweden and Norway had their own winter sport festivals; they wanted no competition from the Olympic Games. A compromise was reached. An "International Sports Week" was to be held in Chamonix from January 25 to February 5.

The designation of the first Winter Olympics would not be confirmed until 1926. Once again, hockey was on the program, the six-man variety this time. In fact, all the Olympic rules were the same as the Canadian Amateur Hockey Association's — except for one. The exception required that the goalie stand erect at all times!

The Toronto Granites were named to represent Canada, and the team, along with two figure skaters, Cecil Eustace-Smith and Melville Rogers, and a speed-skater, Charles Gorman, set sail from Saint John, New Brunswick, on January 11, 1924. It took 11 days by ship and train for the contingent to reach Chamonix, and the hockey players were beginning to lose their edge of conditioning. Alas, warm weather had hit Chamonix, and the ice had turned watery. Practice on skates was out of the question, and the players tried to compensate with days of hiking through the French Alps. Finally the weather turned colder. The teams from Sweden, Finland, and Norway took to the ice for their workouts. When it was Canada's turn to practise, the Scandinavians raised noisy objections. Oh no, they said, the ice was now too fragile. After a round of heavy negotiations, the Canadians settled for a compromise of sorts: they could skate on the curling rink — but without their sticks.

The hockey rink at Chamonix was outdoors under the shadow of Mont Blanc. A huge surface was flooded with water; the best 90-by-185-foot section was enclosed with "boards" six inches high. Behind the goal closest to Mont Blanc, a large screen similar to one behind home plate in a baseball game was erected. That was to protect against the risk that a raised puck would be shot into the snow behind the net and trigger an avalanche.

It was pond hockey for the Canadians. Caps were worn by the players, frontward when attacking the goal towards the sun, backward when away from it. Teams

Although he was an American citizen, boxer Bert Schneider took gold for Canada in 1920. Schneider had lived in Canada since infancy, but was born in Cleveland.

changed ends halfway through the third period, so that each goalie would be affected equally by the glare from the sun.

There were eight teams entered, two divisions created. Canada was in a pool with Czechoslovakia, Sweden, and Switzerland. In the other division were the United States, Belgium, Britain, and France. The two top teams in each division met in the semi-finals, first place playing second to decide the finalists for the gold.

In its first game, Canada met Czechoslovakia. It was no contest. Canada shut them out while scoring 30 goals; Harry Watson netted 13. In the next game, against Sweden, Canada changed goaltenders, Ernie Collett replacing Jack Cameron. It was another shutout, this time by a score of 22–0. The Swiss were the opposition for the third match. They fared no better, losing 33–0. Again, Harry Watson scored 13 goals.

In the other pool, the United States had kept pace. It also had three shutouts: 19–0 over Belgium, 22–0 with the French, and 11–0 in the game with the British. The crossover games would serve to give some indication of the relative strength of the two teams. The United States defeated Sweden 20–0; Canada eliminated Britain 19–2.

Any contest with the Americans was sure to generate excitement because of the natural rivalry of the North American neighbours; it was even more true of this game. The Canadians assumed that if the game ended in a tie, overtime would be played. Not so. A ruling was made that since the Americans had fewer goals scored against them in total — none, to the Canadians' two — their for/against goal ratio was better, and in the event of a tie game, the United States would win the gold medal. The Canadians launched an official protest, to no avail. The ruling stood.

The angry Canadians took to the ice on a bright, sunny day, February 3. The European referee called the two captains to centre ice prior to the game. Some thought he was trying to defuse what appeared to be a tense situation. Instead, the captains were asked their age. Duncan Munro, the Canadian, was 21. The American was 28. The older was given his choice of ends. Nonetheless, it was the Canadians who prevailed by a 6–1 score, Harry Watson having a four-goal game.

For skill and thrills, the game was matchless. Spectators had packed the rink in anticipation of just such a contest. Some stood on the roofs of nearby buildings to watch. Toronto's *Globe* reported that it was the "most brilliant and roughest ice battle ever staged on a European rink." Telegrams poured in from Prime Minister Mackenzie King, Ontario's premier, the Granite Club, and the French Olympic Committee. Baron Pierre de Coubertin himself presented the gold medal on February 5.

The Toronto Granites fought a fierce game in 1924 at Chamonix to take home Canada's second gold medal in hockey.

Beginning with the 1924 Summer Olympics, there was an attempt to streamline the Games. Previously, it had been left to the whims of the organizers to select the events. The 1924 Games saw the international governing bodies assume more responsibility for the conduct of their sports. Most of the federations were European-based. That caused a certain amount of confusion among the North Americans, particularly the Canadians. They were not invited to a meeting of the captains of the various trap-shooting teams and were therefore unaware that in addition to the usual six events, an extra category of "ten birds" launched 80 to 90 yards away from the shooting position was to be included. The inexperience with the new program was enough to remove the Canadian team from gold medal contention. It won the silver. In boxing, where the Canadians had enjoyed so much success in Antwerp, there was only one bronze medal, won by weakened welterweight Doug Lewis; he had had to lose seven pounds in order to make the weight classification. Two other Canadian boxers were unable to qualify because they failed to meet the weight restriction.

Canada won two silvers in the rowing events. The University of Toronto eights, coached by Tom Louden, came second to the United States. There was also a second-place finish for the fours, the Vancouver Boat Club. Circumstances seemed to work against the Canadians. They had a late start, unaware that the race had begun; they thought that the officials were lining up the boats. Unable to hear, they didn't react to the verbal command *"Partez!"* A dropped flag served to jump-start the crew. Rowing furiously, it took them 500 metres to catch up to the others. At the end, their efforts left them short by a boat length.

The Canadians repeated their hockey success at the 1928 Winter Olympics at St. Moritz, Switzerland. The University of Toronto Grads had won the Allan Cup in 1927 under the coaching of Conn Smythe. It had been a banner season for the university; the Intercollegiate team, directed by coach Lester B. "Mike" Pearson, the future prime minister, also won its title the same year. When Smythe was unable to attend the Games — he was busy putting together the NHL expansion New York Rangers —W. A. Hewitt looked after the coaching. He was assisted by 25-year-old Harold Ballard. The future owner of the Toronto Maple Leafs and Hamilton Tiger-Cats was well liked by the members of the team, so much so that at the players' insistence he carried the Canadian flag in the Opening Ceremonies. Even in those years, Ballard was a free spirit. Towards the end of the Games, he cut down the official Olympic flag, hid it among his belongings, and brought it back to Toronto. For years, it decorated one of the walls in his office at Maple Leaf Gardens. Occasionally, he even used it as a bedspread.

Senior amateur hockey was at its peak in 1928 and the Varsity Grads were the *crème de la crème*. Their lineup was somewhat of an oddity with two Sullivan brothers and three Plaxtons. There was absolutely no doubt that they would return with the gold. Some Europeans feared that Canada might be unsporting and roll up huge scores, which could lead to the end of some nations' hockey programs. Hewitt scoffed at this attitude and pushed his players to perform at their highest level.

Hewitt was open to one novel suggestion from the organizers. There were 10 other nations in the tournament. For the first time, the Americans were absent: their hockey association had not paid its dues for the past four years and its team was barred. The remaining teams were organized into three pools. "A" included Great Britain, Hungary, Belgium, and France; "B" had Sweden, Poland, and Czechoslovakia; "C" contained Switzerland, Germany (invited back into the Olympics for the first time since the war), and Austria. Canada was placed by itself. The proposal called for the teams from each pool to play among themselves to determine three winners. Canada would then play each pool champion to determine the gold medal winner.

The compromise proved only that Canada was vastly superior at the sport. In its first game, Canada defeated Sweden 11–0. The Canadian domination was so thorough that goalie Dr. Joe Sullivan skated to the boards at one point to have his picture taken with some spectators while play was in the Swedes' end. The second game was with Great Britain, a team made up of many Canadians. It was a 14–0 victory; the Grads registered an amazing 150 shots on the beleaguered British goalie. Sullivan's stonewalling continued in the third game. The team registered its third shutout, a 13–0 defeat of Switzerland, and took home a gold medal.

The 1928 Summer Games took place in Amsterdam. The International Olympic Committee would have preferred to stage both competitions in the same country, but the absence of a hilly terrain and a suitable climate for the winter festival in Holland made this impossible.

The Amsterdam Olympics were the Games with a difference. The Olympic Flame made its first appearance. There were many changes, and foremost among

The University of Toronto Grads were accompanied to St. Moritz by assistant coach Harold Ballard, where they played three consecutive shutouts to take home a gold medal.

them in the "Roaring Twenties" was the improving status of women, who were permitted to stage their own track and field events for the first time.

Such progressiveness aroused controversy. There were only five women's track and field events: the 100-metre race, the 4 × 100 metre relay, the high jump, discus, and the 800-metre run. Nonetheless, condemnation was voiced by a variety of sources. The Pope was opposed. And the president of the IOC, Pierre de Coubertin, held some of the same reservations. Believing that women could never reach the records set by men, he saw women as hindrances to the Olympic ideal of *Citius, Altius, Fortius* - faster, higher, stronger. He saw a threat to his concept of "brothers in arms," a chivalric athletic élite who were continually pushing back the limits of human achievement. The inclusion of women in the Games was "impractical, uninteresting, unaesthetic and, we are not afraid to add, wrong." The public exhibition of women on the athletic field was "undignified." The controversy was such that the members of the IOC were required to vote on the issue. But when the ballots were counted, women's track and field was supported by a majority.

Despite having voted against their inclusion, Canada sent its own team of women, "the matchless six," to compete among the 40 nations. Not only did the team compete, it performed the best of all of the women. The six chosen were Myrtle Cook, a 26-year-old sprinter from Toronto; Ethel Smith, 21, another sprinter from Toronto; runner Fanny "Bobbie" Rosenfeld, 23, an all-round athlete, born in Russia but a Canadian citizen since 1920, and later selected Canada's Outstanding Female Athlete for the first 50 years of the twentieth century; Ethel Catherwood, high jumper, 19, born in Hannah, North Dakota, but a resident of Saskatoon since childhood; Jean Thompson, 17, from Penetanguishene, Ontario, entered in the 800 metres; and Florence Bell, 18, a sprinter from Toronto.

The six were selected after special trials held for women competitors in Halifax. Some soul searching had to be done by two of the six. Ethel Smith and Myrtle Cook were each engaged to be married, and their wedding dates had been set. The postponement of the weddings caused the media to praise the women's "fine sense of sportsmanship." Their spouses-to-be were characterized as having the "patience of Job."

Canada's "Matchless Six", front two rows, outperformed all other female track and field athletes at the 1928 Summer Games in Amsterdam.

37

Outfitted in white pleated flannel skirts, white silk stockings and blouses, scarlet shoes and hats, and white blazers trimmed with red piping, the women joined the men's group and left Toronto's Union Station on July 10 by train for Montreal. From there they sailed on the SS *Albertic* on July 11.

The first event held in women's track and field was the 100-metre race. Canada qualified three finalists: Myrtle Cook, Fanny Rosenfeld, and Ethel Smith. But Cook and German runner Leni Schmidt were disqualified in the final for false starts. When the event was finally run and completed, three runners appeared to be tied at the finish line. Judges disagreed among themselves as to who was first. Discussion grew animated. In the end, Elizabeth Robinson of the United States was declared the winner in a time of 12.2 seconds. Rosenfeld was placed second, Smith, third. Their time was given as 12.3. The Canadians were upset. Rosenfeld had already defeated Robinson in the semi-finals. Canadian officials, aware that Rosenfeld had been inhibited by Myrtle Cook's disqualification, protested. They wanted the event to be rerun. To no avail: the judges' decision was final.

There was a measure of some justification in Canadian women's performance in the 4 × 100-metre relay. Rosenfeld, Smith, Cook, and Bell won the gold in a world's record time of 48.4. They beat the United States by four-tenths of a second. Myrtle Cook won a moral victory of sorts; she was matched in the anchor leg with Elizabeth Robinson, outrunning her to cinch the gold medal.

Fanny "Bobbie" Rosenfeld, Canada's premier woman athlete of her generation, won a controversial silver in a tight finish to the 100 m sprint at Amsterdam. She was also lead runner in the 4 x 100 m relay team that took a record-setting gold medal.

Myrtle Cook crosses the finish line first in a qualifying heat at the 1928 Amsterdam Games.

A second gold medal was won in the high jump. Ethel Catherwood set an Olympic record of 1.59 metres. In winning, she captured a nation's imagination. Newspaper accounts delighted in describing her as a "dream in repose," "as retiring as a morning glory," "a sweetheart in action," "the western gazelle," the "Saskatoon Lily," and the "most photographed girl at the Games." The Canadian team also picked up a fourth (Jean Thompson) and fifth (Rosenfeld) in the 800 metres. Thompson had been favoured to do better, but she injured her leg during the week and was bedridden, unable to maintain her conditioning. This 800-metre race caused a review of women's track and field after the Games were over. It was the longest event for women. Some who entered were not adequately trained, collapsing before or after they reached the finish line. Once again, a vote was taken on the future of women's track and field events at the Olympics. Once more, Canada voted against their inclusion; once more, the naysayers were outvoted. The 800 metres, the 200 metres, the long jump, and shotput were all eliminated for women, leaving only the 100 metre, 4 × 100-metre relay, high jump, discus, javelin, and 80-metre hurdles.

The 1928 Olympics represented a high point for Canada. Using a point basis of six for first through to one for sixth place, Canada finished fourth of 45 nations with a total of 55 points. It had been sixteenth in 1924. Percy Williams of Vancouver showed the way with gold medals in the 100-metre and 200-metre events. James Ball was

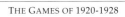

The 1928 Olympics were a high point for Canadian track and field athletes. Silver was taken in the 400 m race by James Ball.

Phil Edwards would earn five medals during his Olympic career. His first, a bronze, came in the 4 x 400 m relay in 1928.

only inches short of a gold in the 400 metres. The foursome of Alex Wilson, Phil Edwards, Stan Glover, and James Ball won a bronze in the 4 × 400-metre relay. For Phil Edwards, it was the first of five medals that he would win over three Olympics. He also finished fourth in the 800-metre finals.

In the double sculls rowing event, Canada entered for the first time. Joe Wright and John Guest rowed to a silver medal. The Argonaut Rowing Club's eights also won a bronze. There was a bronze in boxing, welterweight Ray Smillie placing third. Jim Trifunov also won a bronze in bantamweight wrestling. He had not been funded by the Canadian Olympic Committee; the citizens of Regina had paid his expenses and their generosity was rewarded when he won the medal. Two other medals were earned in wrestling: Maurice Letchford gained a bronze in the welterweight category, and Don Stockton was a silver medallist among the middleweights. A swimming bronze was also won in the 4 × 200-metre relay: Munroe Bourne, Garnet Ault, Jim Thompson, and Walter Spence formed the team. In the demonstration sport of lacrosse, Canada, Great Britain, and the United States all finished tied in first place to share the gold medal.

Amsterdam set a new benchmark for Canadians in the Summer Games: five golds, four silvers, and seven bronzes. It was an exciting finish to an exciting decade in Canadian amateur sport.

Toronto's Argo Eights had a long tradition of wins when the rowing team took home bronze in 1928.

Profile

Percy Williams

GOLD MEDALLIST,
100-METRE AND 200-METRE SPRINTS, 1928

Percy Williams was born May 19, 1908, in Vancouver, British Columbia. His father was a streetcar conductor; his mother worked as a cashier in a movie theatre. While Percy was still a young boy, his parents separated, and he went to live with his mother. Growing up, he was diagnosed with rheumatic fever and doctors suggested that he not engage in strenuous activities. The doctor's advice was one thing; peer pressure was another. Williams got involved in school sports because, as he recollected, "you were a bum if you didn't compete." In 1926, during the summer when he celebrated his eighteenth birthday, Williams caught the eye of Tom Granger, a coach in search of an athlete. Granger's current protégé was Vancouver sprint champion Wally Scott. Williams and Scott raced to a draw. Granger saw more than the tie in Williams; he saw raw talent, which he thought he could develop into a world champion. There was work to be done; Williams's running style was awkward, all legs, no arm motion, but his determination was unstoppable.

If Williams was somewhat unique in style, Granger was absolutely unorthodox in his approach to training. There was to be no more swimming for Williams. All available time was to be spent on the track working on form. Recognizing that the five-foot, six-inch, 125-pound Williams had a fragile constitution, Granger decided to forgo typical energy-sapping training. Williams would concentrate on starts, develop explosiveness. Granger set up mattresses on one side of a room. Williams would crouch on the opposite side, then burst on command into the mattress to cushion himself from injury. Between races, Williams lay in his dressing room warmed by a covering of blankets, his muscles gaining the time to repair and to absorb the benefits of warming up without being drained of energy. In cold weather, he was rubbed with coconut oil and dressed in layers of track suits and sweaters to retain his body heat. Granger also arranged to give Williams a training partner. The fellow competitor was granted a head start, sometimes up to 10 yards, which gave Williams the motivation to shift to another level of acceleration after his initial explosive start.

During the Olympics, Granger gave specific instructions to Williams's roommate, Harry Warren. Williams had the habit of pulling the sheet over his head just before he fell asleep. Aghast at the thought that his protégé would suffer a lack of oxygen, Granger instructed Warren to stay awake and pull the sheet back from Williams's head.

For the Olympics, Williams travelled with the Canadian team to Amsterdam, while the ever-dedicated Granger made his way to the Games at his own expense, arriving three days after the team. Immediately he set about arranging Williams's training schedule. He installed a mattress in the room shared by Williams and Warren, not for anyone to sleep on but for Williams to practise his driving starts. Day and night, Granger camped in the hall outside the runners' room. If an idea about training or strategy struck him, he slipped a note under their door.

Williams's fragile appearance was misleading. At the Games, Dutch doctors gathered statistics on all the competitors — some 3,000 athletes — measurements of chest, waist, biceps, thighs, calves, chest expansion, and all-round strength. The medical conclusion was that, of all the Olympians gathered in Amsterdam, Percy Williams was the one "perfect athlete."

In the first heat for the 100-metre run, Williams could afford to coast home in a relatively leisurely 11:0 seconds and still finish first. He stepped things up against better competition in the second and third heats, registering a solid 10:6. In the semi-finals, Williams got off to a slow start. The starting holes — there were no blocks at the time — were too giving, and Williams was back on his haunches when the starter fired his pistol. Behind from the beginning, he came within a whisker of nipping the American Bob McAllister and finished second. Next day, in the gold medal race, Williams refused to be rattled by two false starts. When the gun finally sounded the legitimate start,

Williams broke into a lead that he never relinquished. He took the gold medal and with it the designation "world's fastest human."

A few hours after his triumph, Williams returned to his hotel. A huge crowd surrounded it. "What's happening?" Williams asked. When someone told him that everybody was waiting for the amazing Canadian sprinter, Williams decided to join, anonymously, the crowd of waiting admirers. "So I'm supposed to be the world champ," he later wrote in his diary. "Crushed apples! No more fun now."

Worried that the 100-metre event had drained Williams's strength, Olympic officials offered to withdraw him from the 200-metre race. No thanks, Williams said. He finished first in the initial two heats, running 21:6 to equal the Olympic record in the second. In the finals, Williams's eighth race in four days, he exploded out of his start, accelerated, hit his stride, and shifted into his final kick to beat the other runners to the tape in 21:8. It was Percy Williams's second gold medal, and his two victories represent the only time, to this day, that a Canadian has ever won the 100 metres and 200 metres at the Olympic Games.

Percy Williams is hoisted by ecstatic teammates. After his double Olympic win, Williams clinched his dominance by going unbeaten in a spectacular U.S. series of indoor races against the world's top runners.

CHAPTER THREE

OLYMPIC PLENTY in a DECADE of DEPRESSION

THE GAMES OF 1932-1936

WILLIAM HUMBER

AT THE TIME THE 1932 WINTER OLYMPICS WERE AWARDED TO LAKE Placid in Upper New York State and the same year's Summer Olympics to Los Angeles, it was still the Roaring Twenties. The world's economy was on an upward spiral, and organizers anticipated the most glorious Games ever in the most affluent of nations. But when 1932 rolled around, the entire world, and particularly industrial countries like the United States, had fallen into the deepest trough of what was to be a decade-long depression. It was a measure of American ingenuity that the economically burdened United States pulled off both sets of Games, especially the more demanding Summer Olympiad, with style, efficiency, and even glamour.

The Winter Games had a distinct Canadian flavour beginning, curiously enough, with the snow. Truckloads of white stuff had to be brought down to Lake Placid from north of the border to repair the cross-country skiing tracks.

On the competitive front, Canada was particularly outstanding in men's speed-skating. In the 500 metres, Canadians finished third (Alex Hurd), fourth (Frank Stack), and fifth (William Logan). They were even better in the 1,500 metres: second (Hurd), third (Logan), and fourth (Stack). And in the 5,000 metres, Logan got a bronze, and Stack came through with another bronze in the 10,000 metres. Frank Stack, a remarkably durable skater, qualified for the 1936 Games. Alas, Canada couldn't afford to send him to Germany, where the

Winter Olympics were held that year, but amazingly he was still around to compete in the skating events at the Games of both 1948 and 1952. Montgomery Wilson took bronze in figure skating, earning Canada's first-ever medal in this sport.

In hockey, Canada once again took gold, but they didn't breeze through

Skating has long been prime medal territory for Canadians. Speed-skater Frank Stack (above) was a durable Olympic competitor who skated to a fourth in the 1932 500 m race, and participated again in 1948 and 1952. Montgomery Wilson (right) earned Canada's first figure skating medal, a bronze, at Lake Placid.

the opposition as they had at past Games. Indeed, the Canadians, represented by a team from Winnipeg, found all they could handle in the Americans. In a preliminary game, Canada edged the United States 2–1. Then, in the tournament's final game, the Canadians and the Americans were once again matched. If Canada, undefeated, won, the gold was theirs. If the United States, with just the single loss, won, the Americans would force an extra and deciding game. The match turned into a thriller, going into three overtime periods before ending in a 2–2 tie. That gave Canada the gold medal by the narrow margin of the one-goal victory over the United States in the opening game.

Canadian speed-skater Jean Wilson also beat the Americans. This came in the 500-metre race, a demonstration event at these Games, and Wilson took first place over two powerful American rivals. Wilson's prize was not a gold medal, but rather a free trip to Japan. Sadly, she was never able to make the trip because she came down with a rare muscular disease that claimed her life a year after the Olympics.

Canadian mushers came to the fore at Lake Placid when Emil St. Godard of The Pas, Manitoba, drove his well-conditioned huskies first across the finish line in the 50-mile demonstration dog-sled event. His team had raced up to 1,500 miles a season, but he was a remarkably sensitive driver who had pulled out of a big race in Prince Albert, Saskatchewan, in 1927 because, as he said, "I am not going to bleed my dogs to win a prize. There is blood every yard of that course."

The organizers of the Los Angeles Games faced problems far greater than those of their Lake Placid countrymen. The Summer Games are longer, involve more events, and attract more countries and participants. Los Angeles's location added to the travel burden of Europeans. The city had been awarded the Games in 1923, and a huge coliseum seating 100,000 was built. By 1930, the world financial situation led to open talk about abandoning the '32 Games until conditions improved. It was characteristic of those Games' magic that L.A. mayor William Garland, appearing before the Olympic Congress in Berlin in the summer of 1930, proposed a bold plan under which the local committee would provide an Olympic village to feed, house, entertain, and locally transport each individual athlete for $2 a day. Reservations began to trickle in, and by the time the games began, over 1,500 competitors from 34 countries were in Los Angeles.

Women's speed-skating was a demonstration event at the 1932 Games, where Canadian Jean Wilson set records in both the 500m and the 1,500 m races.

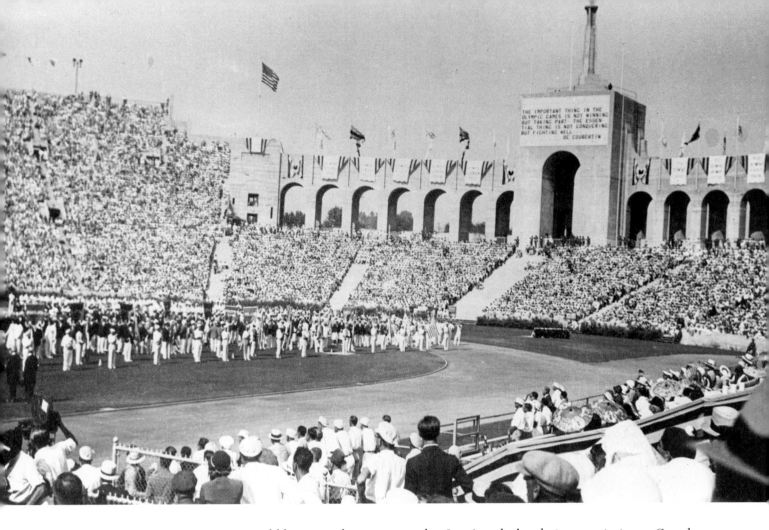

THE IMPORTANT THING IN THE OLYMPIC GAMES IS NOT WINNING BUT TAKING PART. THE ESSENTIAL THING IS NOT CONQUERING BUT FIGHTING WELL. DE COUBERTIN

The Los Angeles Summer Games were the most lavish the world had ever seen, and their glamour was heightened by the contrast with the increasing misery of the Depression.

It would be a mistake to assume that Los Angeles's relative proximity to Canada made it easy for Canadian participation. The depressed economic conditions in Canada meant a severe reduction in government money for athletes' training and travel expenses. Swimmer Betty Edwards later recalled, "We all had to get involved in fund-raising. At our meets in Toronto we'd go up into the crowd with a pot full of change and shake it hoping to collect money from spectators. I hated it." While it had been agreed that eight boxers would make the trip, there was train fare for only four, so the whole team staged a series of exhibition matches to raise money. It was a good thing too, because one of the fighters eventually won a gold medal.

Will Rogers was the first of many Hollywood celebrities to salute the Canadian delegation. Of their debut in the Opening Ceremonies he wrote, "Best showing at the opening was by Canada, second by Italy, third Argentine." The *Los Angeles Times* said of the Canadian team in their bright red jackets, "Canada's contingent drew the biggest cheer from the assembled multitude. Appears that instead of ex-Iowans, Southern California must be either pro-Canadian or ex-Canadian." They were quickly dubbed the "Crimson Canucks." Canadian rower Ned Pratt, an eventual bronze medallist in the double sculls, recalled that the entire stadium was filled, "except for an area taken up by John Barrymore and W.C. Fields and some others. Their drinking habits were considered raucous and it was found necessary to isolate them."

It might have appeared that the Canadians were one big happy family, but an acrimonious dispute behind the scenes threatened one of Canada's best medal hopes. At the time, Duncan McNaughton of Canada was, along with Bob Van Osdel and Cornelius Johnson of the United States and Simeon Toribio of the Philippines, one of the four best high jumpers in the world. The four were all attending school in the Los Angeles area and had often competed against one another prior to the Games. McNaughton, from British Columbia, was attending the University of Southern California on a track scholarship, but he had not participated in the Canadian trials. The only cost for the Canadian team would be the daily $2 stipend to house him in the Olympic Village for the few days of his event, but his participation wasn't guaranteed.

"I'd been disqualified for diving over the bar in the 1930 British Empire Games in Hamilton and a lot of Canadian officials weren't too happy with me," McNaughton later said. "Anyway, they told me I'd have to meet the Canadian standard of six feet two inches to qualify for the Olympic team. I thought this was a little ridiculous as I'd been clearing that height all year in competition and so I told them to stuff it.... In any case I didn't know until the day before the Olympic event whether I'd be in the high jump or not."

According to the official British Olympic Association report of the Games, McNaughton got his place only after finally jumping six feet three inches in a tryout after the rest of the Canadian team reached Los Angeles.

"I had some obvious advantages," he recalled. "I was on home turf, having competed perhaps 10 times in the Coliseum, and of course I was living in the area. Nevertheless, I had some problems. A German jumper in front of me was a meticulous fellow like the ones we'd encounter later in the war, and he'd check and re-check the bar. I figure if you're going to jump, get on with it. I was glad to see him fall out. Still I was having trouble clearing the lower heights. I was using the western roll and jumping off my right foot. My friend and rival in this event, Bob Van Osdel, told me to get more kick in my left leg."

The advice worked, but the four California neighbours were tied at six feet, five and ⅝ inches, and none could go higher. A jump-off was held and the well-conditioned Canadian outlasted his rivals for the gold. It was the first time since the 1906 Intercalated Games that a non-American had won the event.

Duncan McNaughton is the only Canadian man ever to earn a gold medal in high jump.

Movie star Norma Shearer poses with members of the Canadian Olympic Women's Swim team at the 1932 Games.

The sheer scope of the Games, the immensity of the Coliseum, and the comradeship of the Olympic Village earned the L.A. Games recognition as the first of the modern-style Games, but much of their glamour and popularity came from Hollywood. For the first time, celebrity and Olympic athleticism were allied. There was no better symbol of this marriage than a party recalled by Canadian fencer Joan Archibald Riddell. "I only won one of three bouts and was out of the competition early so that gave me time to see what was going on. I was shown around by Norma Shearer, who at the time was a big name in the movies. I was a good friend of her cousin in Montreal. I was chosen as the lucky guest to meet the famous Barrymores — chosen because they were such keen swordsmen and I was the only female fencer from Canada."

Hollywood took to the Canadians with passion perhaps because many had roots in the land to the north. One was Toronto-born Mary Pickford, who with husband Douglas Fairbanks welcomed Canadians to her estate.

Similar encounters are recalled by Ray Lewis who, along with Phil Edwards, James Ball, and Alex Wilson, won a bronze in the 4 × 400-metre track relay. Lewis and Edwards were among the scattering of black athletes who competed in these Games. "During the competition there was a lull in the action, and we went down to a box where the movie stars were sitting and asked for their autographs. When they heard we were from Canada they asked for ours. So *I* signed for Gary Cooper."

Lewis, a lifetime Hamiltonian, had persevered against extraordinary odds. He worked as a railway porter on the transcontinental train, about the only well-paid job available for blacks in those days, and he remembered, "We'd go from Vancouver to Chicago and deadhead home from there. There was a lot of single track and sometimes we'd stop for a few hours while repairs were underway. That's when I got in my practice, jogging up and down the line. A lot of farmers must have wondered what this crazy guy was doing."

Canada's other Olympic gold medal was provided by a bantamweight boxer (118 pounds) and former jockey, Horace "Lefty" Gwynne, who defeated Vito Melis of Italy, José Villanueva from the Philippines, and a German, Hans Ziglarski. "I got my start during the first war," Gwynne later said. "My dad had returned to England to join the British Army, and the brigadier had my brother and me put on a boxing show for the troops. We were just kids and they billed us as the Gwynne midgets. I was going to become a jockey but put on too much weight, so I went back into boxing. It was the sportswriter Lou Marsh who gave me my nickname. He said I couldn't go into the ring with a name like Horace. He asked if I had any habits. I told him I was left-handed, and he hung the name on me."

Bantamweight boxer Horace Gwynne won one of Canada's two gold medals at Los Angeles.

In other events, it was an era of great Canadian middle-distance runners. Among Canada's achievements were Alex Wilson's bronze in the 400-metre track event, and silver in the 800 metres, followed in that race by Phil Edwards, who duplicated his bronze in the 1,500 metres. Percy Williams, Canada's double gold medal winner in 1928, narrowly missed a bronze in the 4 × 100-metre relay. Hilda Strike was nipped at the wire by Poland's Stanislawa Walasiewicz in the women's 100-metre final, a result made poignant many years later by the discovery on her death that the Polish athlete was, at least anatomically, a man. A clumsy pass denied the Canadian women a gold in the 4 × 100-metre relay, and Hilda Strike went home with two silvers.

Canada's oarsmen won a bronze in one of the country's historically popular events, the eights, and Noel de Mille and Ned Pratt earned the same honour in the double sculls event. Dan MacDonald took silver in a less favoured event, welterweight wrestling. Eva Dawes was third in the women's high jump. Canadians also won medals in yachting, though Ronald Maitland's silver aboard the *Santa Maria* in the eight-metre class was made easier by the entry of only two boats in that class.

While the stardust of Hollywood may have cast a lasting glow on the Los Angeles Games, a more sinister force was arising in Europe that threatened the staging of the 1936 Games and forever changed the apolitical image of sport.

Two Canadians, silver medallist Alex Wilson (left) and bronze medallist Phil Edwards flank Great Britain's Tom Hampson, who came first in the 800 m run.

In 1932 at an International Olympic Committee meeting in Barcelona, a German delegation led by Dr. Theodor Lewald and Carl Diem representing the democratic Weimar Republic was awarded the 1936 Summer Olympics for the city of Berlin. Germany had been scheduled to hold the 1916 Games, but war disrupted those plans. Events a few months after the awarding of the '36 Games would once again threaten Germany's plans. In January 1933 the Nazi party of Adolf Hitler came to power in Germany. In 1932, he had called the Olympics "an invention of Jews and freemasons" and "a play inspired by Judaism which cannot possibly be put on in a Reich ruled by National Socialists." Hitler was disturbed by Theodor Lewald's part-Jewish ancestry, and for a time it was believed Germany would simply abandon the Olympic commitment.

In the fall of 1933, however, on a visit to the proposed site, Hitler was swept up by the possibilities of the occasion. "The stadium must be built by the Reich," he proclaimed. "It will be the task of the nation. If Germany is to stand host to the entire world, her preparations must be complete and magnificent."

The top three finishers in the women's 100 m race were separated by only a tenth of a second, with Canada's Hilda Strike earning silver against Poland's Stanislawa Walasiewicz—who was later revealed to be a man. Third place went to American Wilhelmina von Bremen.

From this point on, the Games went forward as part of Nazi Germany's greater propaganda campaign to convince the world of its impressive might. In the rest of the world, a furious debate ensued on the morality of sending athletes to a nation whose political leaders formed policy on the basis of racism and militarism. The opponents of participation lost the struggle, though their fears would eventually be tragically affirmed.

In Canada, the forces of ambivalence were victorious. Speaking in the House of Commons in the early part of 1936, Prime Minister Mackenzie King said, "It is doubtful that anyone participating in the Olympic Games is a representative of the Government of this country." By such odd logic, it was deemed inappropriate for the government to intervene in any decision by Canadian Olympic officials on Canadian participation. As a result, in early February, a Canadian team was on its way to the German Winter Olympic site in Garmisch-Partenkirchen.

Canadians can be divided by many things, but one obsession unites them from coast to coast — the fate of their ice hockey reputation. The real story of the 1936 Winter Olympics should have been the German decision to invite the Jewish ice

The 1936 Winter Games marked the only time that a Canadian hockey team failed to take gold between 1920 and 1952. Canadian officials charged that the winning British team was manned by "shamateurs" who had played professionally in Canada.

hockey star Rudi Ball to return home from Spain and play for the German national team. "The Nazis are disgusted," said the *London Daily Sketch* on February 5, "because a Jew is included, and the Jews because Ball accepted." In Canada, however, the only story was the composition of Great Britain's team, which included two hockey stars, goaltender James Foster and forward Alex Archer, who, though born in Britain, had emigrated at an early age to Canada. They had learned their skills on Canadian ice and returned to England without permission of the Canadian Amateur Hockey Association (CAHA) to play in London's popular circuit of semi-pro hockey.

"Foster may be an amateur," Mike Rodden, a referee and *Globe* writer, said, "but it is known, or, at least, has been alleged, that when he was a member of the Moncton Hawks, every player on that team received $3,000 a year. …Therefore, it is remarkable that Foster should be a party to the Olympic oath of amateurism." It was a concern of little interest to British Ice Hockey Association secretary J.F. (Bunny) Ahearne, who would himself be a thorn in the side of future Canadian attempts to circumvent international ice hockey amateur rules.

E.A. Gilroy, president of the CAHA, declared that "hockey in Great Britain, as conducted by the British Ice Hockey Association, is a racket." The Canadians had the upper hand in the dispute and the two players' suspension could not be revoked without their assent. Ultimately, the Canadian authorities withdrew their protest. Such magnanimity was no doubt due to a Canadian conviction that no other team, particularly a British one, could ever upset a lineup of bona fide Canadians.

On February 11, 1936, the first blow to Canadian ice hockey prestige in this century was dealt when English goalie Jimmy Foster stoned the Canadians in the opening game, giving Great Britain a 2–1 victory despite the fact that the Canadians had 80 percent of play.

More shocking to the Canadians was a realization that teams advancing to the final round were not required to play teams they had defeated. The Brits had a free path to the gold medal, assuming no one else beat them. Most Canadians realized that the Canadian team was made up largely of members of the 1935 Allan Cup runners-up from Port Arthur, Ontario, with a few reinforcements. It was not an all-star amateur lineup and had none of the country's best professionals. To the rest of the world, however, they wore the Canadian label, and that inspired awe, particularly among those like the Hungarians, who lost 15–0 to the Canucks. At the same time, Canadian officials were stymied in their attempt to change the rules for the final stage of competition and proclaimed loudly that Canada would quit the Olympic hockey series.

On the sidelines of this disagreement were the Germans. They had used the Winter Games as a prelude to the more visible Summer Games. Clumsy Nazi officiousness was employed in blocking off cordons to allow for the arrival and departure of Hitler; Hermann Goering and Joseph Goebbels were noted by visitors. Hundreds of camouflaged army trucks careered about the site, and brutal S.S. Guards roamed the streets, often terrorizing visitors with unexplained manoeuvres and silly commands.

Against such a backdrop and now aware there would be no rule change to accommodate their hopes in a final round, the Canadians entered their game with Germany in a foul mood. Before a crowd that included Goebbels and Goering and 10,000 German fans encouraged by three years of propaganda to consider themselves a master race, the Canadians, in the muted language of the *Toronto Globe*, "dropped the gentleness that had marked earlier games and gave the German team, the German populace and German Government officials a lesson in the art of bodychecking. The bumps are perfectly legal but the opposing hockeymen didn't like them and neither did the pro-German crowd."

"At one time," said the *Globe* of February 14 in reference to the German fans, "the demonstration was so pronounced Paul Joseph Goebbels, German Minister for Propaganda, arose in the official box and motioned for the crowd to cease." Canada beat the Germans 6–2 but never again met the British in the competition and was reduced to a silver medal finish.

The Germans learned much from the Winter Olympic experience and sought a somewhat more benign image for their Summer Games. They introduced the now popular lighting of the Olympic Flame at Olympia in Greece and its 2,000-mile relay to Berlin. German composer Richard Strauss wrote a hymn for the Opening Ceremonies. The Games organization, characterized by detailed, almost minute-by-minute thoroughness, irritated at least one British observer who wrote, with prescient clarity, "The whole organization was one vast machine, a machine which lacked a little the human touch so desirable in international meetings."

Aside from Adolf Hitler's obvious presence, the 1936 Summer Games in Berlin belonged largely to two people. One was Leni Riefenstahl, who a few years earlier had romanticized and attempted to immortalize the Nazi regime with her brilliant film *Triumph of the Will* and now filmed the Games for similar propaganda purposes. The other was black American athlete Jesse Owens, whose response to Hitler's master race theorizing was four gold medals, thus effectively forcing Hitler to abandon

The 1936 Berlin Olympics were a grandiose orgy of nationalism for Adolf Hitler's Nazi party.

Kanada

Future president of the Canadian Olympic Association James Worrall, a track and field athlete, was flag-bearer for the Berlin Games.

his practice of publicly congratulating each winner.

The Nazis tried mightily to keep a tight control on the Games, but even their ruthless efficiency could not totally eliminate youthful high jinks by the visiting athletes. One such episode, involving the Olympic flag, was witnessed by Canadian swimmer Bill Puddy. "Two Canadians" —Puddy was reluctant to reveal names — "had gone into Berlin near the end of the Games, had a few beers, and returned near sundown. It was a misty day and the streets of the Olympic Village were empty. The Olympic flag was flying near the Hindenburg Hall, and the two guys wondered what would happen if they loosened the halyards. It was a prank but on release the wet flag came tumbling down. They wrapped it up and ran for it.

"Everyone wanted to cut up a piece as a keepsake but the two Canadians said you'd have to fight them for it. By now there were rumours that Canadians had stolen it, so the two guys put it in a paper bag and went into downtown Berlin to the Wilhelmstrasse railroad station, bought a cheap cardboard suitcase and mailed the flag to their cabin in the Canadian boat, the SS *Montcalm*, the ship the team would sail home on in a month's time. When the two guys arrived at the boat's departure point in Greenwich, the suitcase, with the flag, was in their room." The flag is still in Canadian possession and made a public appearance at least once during events leading up to the 1976 Olympics in Montreal.

Canada's lone gold medallist of these Games, the canoeist Francis Amyot, was a hero of the first order. In 1933 he went to the rescue of three football players, including Dave Sprague, an all-Canadian great, who had tumbled out of their canoe and were in danger of being swept to an almost certain death over the wild Deschênes Rapids. Amyot paddled furiously to their side, and they hung on to his canoe while he fought the current until help arrived.

Amyot and his supporters had had to finance his trip to Berlin. The world's best canoeists were generally Europeans, but in the "One-Seater Canadian" event, Amyot was tactically brilliant. He went out to an early lead, forcing the race favourite, Bohuslav Karlik of Czechoslovakia, to expend considerable energy in the middle of the 1,000-metre event to catch and slightly pass the

German movie director Leni Riefenstahl's film of the Berlin Games has become a film classic.

Canoeist Francis Amyot (opposite) was the sole Canadian gold medallist of the 1936 Summer Games; he also coached and managed the first Canadian Olympic canoeing team.

Canadian. Refusing to falter, Amyot increased his pace. His Czech rival appeared to panic. His rushed stroke became uneven and Amyot caught him with 50 metres to go and paddled to a decisive victory with a time of 5:32.1. Fellow Canadian canoeists Harvey Charters and Frank Saker completed Canada's surprise showing, winning silver in the Two-Seater Canadian 10,000-metre course and a bronze in the Two-Seater Canadian 1,000-metre event.

On a darker side, Irving "Toots" Meretsky went to Berlin as not only a member of the Canadian basketball team (which took a silver medal) but one of the few Jewish athletes in the entire Games. "We took the train from Paris to Germany," he later recalled, " and I met a Jewish traveller on board. He told me not to leave the village at night, not to look at German girls, and not to go to the bars. I followed his advice." Still, Meretsky wasn't prepared to completely ignore the wishes of friends and family back home. "I had some addresses of people to look up and visited a Jewish neighbourhood. No one was on the streets, and the shades were drawn. I knocked at a few doors and was

American track and field superstar Jesse Owens took four gold medals at the Berlin Games: 100m, 200m, broad jump, and 400 m relay.

finally let in. They offered tea and cake. I left some things but it was obvious they were all scared. Hitler had cleared out the villages two or three years before and waited until after the Olympics to clear out the cities."

Canadians had their small moments of glory at the Games. There was John Loaring's silver medal in the 400-metre hurdles; a bronze by Phil Edwards in the 800 metres; the sixth place in the pole vault by Syl Apps, the future Toronto Maple Leaf hockey star; a third place that the women's 4 × 100-metre relay team won after the Germans, leading the race, dropped a baton; a third-place photo finish in the women's 80-metre hurdles by Betty Taylor; and Joe Schleimer's bronze medal in welterweight wrestling.

These made a slim record, an essentially disappointing Games for the Canadian Olympians. But the larger question that faced Canada and all the other competing nations in Berlin was whether the Games themselves would survive Hitler and the Nazis. The answer, ultimately, was yes, but 12 years passed, and a world war was fought, before the Games resumed. When they did, it seemed that somewhere along the line the spirit of Olympian innocence had been changed forever.

Profile

Dr. Phil Edwards

BRONZE MEDALLIST, RUNNING, 1928,
1932(3 MEDALS), AND 1936

Wearing Canada's colours in 21 races from the 1928 Olympics through those of 1936, Dr. Phil Edwards was eliminated from competition only once, and that was in 1928 in the 400-metre semi-final after two first places in preceding heats.

Edwards was born in Georgetown, British Guiana, in 1907. His family was among the local black élite of this British colony, and Edwards studied and ran track at New York University in 1927. As a British subject of a country with no Olympic

Phil Edwards and his bronze medal-winning relay teammates leave the field at the Amsterdam Games.

representation, he had several options and chose to join the Canadian team because he could continue his New York studies. He won a bronze in Amsterdam as a member of Canada's 4 x 400-metre relay team.

If there was some opportunism in Edwards's initial choice, it was no longer an issue in the 1930s as he became first a medical student at McGill University, then the esteemed captain of Canada's Summer Olympic track team, and eventually a respected specialist in tropical diseases and a member of Canada's armed forces.

Edwards was at his peak in the 1932 Games. He reached the finals in all of his events, the 800 metres, 1,500 metres, and the 4 x 400-metre relay and won bronze in each of them. In the 800, he set a torrid pace, one that had already earned him the

Phil Edwards runs in a qualifying heat at the Los Angeles Olympics, where he earned triple bronzes.

nickname of "Old Rabbit." He led at the halfway point and appeared to be increasing the lead, but at the final turn he was caught by his countryman Alex Wilson and by Tom Hampson from Great Britain. Those two raced together stride by stride with the Englishman barely crossing the finish line in first, though both broke the world's record.

Likewise in the 1,500 metres, Edwards and the American favourite, Glenn Cunningham, opened up a huge lead. On the back straight of the last lap, Edwards extended the lead but in a pattern that now marked his running career, an Italian, Luigi Beccali, passed him in the final 100 yards and then John Cornes of Great Britain beat him at the finish line for the silver medal.

"Phil was a natural athlete," recalled Jim Worrall, one of his McGill colleagues and Canadian teammates, and a future IOC executive member. "I don't know how much coaching he got. There was no one else in Canada who knew as much about middle-distance running as Phil. He ran according to his own method of training and knowledge of tactics. He went out fast, got the lead, and tried to hold on. His legs were disproportionately long for his body, and when he accelerated, his body seemed to slump, with his hip level going down two or three inches as he opened up his stride."

By 1936, when Edwards was approaching his thirtieth birthday, his tremendous drive was beginning to fade, but he maintained his competitive schedule, once again entering the 800- and 1,500-metre events and maintaining his place on the 4 x 400-metre relay team.

The 1,500-metre event in Berlin was one of the great races of all time ("magnificent beyond description," said the official British report) with the favourites including Jack Lovelock from New Zealand, Sydney Wooderson from Great Britain, as well as Cunningham and the three medallists from 1932. Wooderson was injured in the heats, but the final was still a classic. Edwards couldn't summon the same breakaway speed of four years before, but at one point in the second lap when Lovelock found himself dangerously boxed, a word to Edwards was all that was needed for the gallant Canadian to let him through. It may have been the difference in the New Zealander's memorable victory as he ran away from Cunningham.

Edwards's best shot at a gold medal was the 800-metre race and he led after a slow first lap. His chief rival, American John Woodruff, caught and passed him, but on the back straight Edwards returned to the lead, and the two raced grimly together to the top of the home stretch. "There was a moment or two," Jim Worrall recalled, "when all you saw was one torso and what appeared to be four legs running under it, and then Woodruff pulled away."

It was Edwards's last competitive Olympics and his teammates showed their affection for him on the way home. Bill Puddy recalled later that the team checked into a Canadian-owned hotel in London prior to their return to Canada. "We were all tired, having just come across the Channel by boat. I was in the tub on the third floor soaking and I heard someone running down the hall and yelling 'Get on your clothes, we're leaving.' There were about 50 or 60 of us out on the street with our bags and that's when I learned that the hotel hadn't allowed Phil to register because he was black. Finally a Canadian official told us that it was sorted out. Phil was going in and so were we."

Edwards joined Canada's armed forces in the Second World War and was stationed in British Columbia near the Pacific theatre, where his knowledge of tropical medicine was invaluable. After the war, he worked with the Olympic team of British Guiana for whom he had competed, despite his move to Canada, in the 1930 and 1934 British Empire Games (winning gold in the 880 yards in 1934). In 1936 he was the first-ever recipient of the Lou Marsh trophy recognizing Canada's premier athlete and was later inducted into New York University's Hall of Fame a year before his death in Montreal in 1971.

URILE OL
SINKI FIN
3. VII

CHAPTER FOUR

THE POSTWAR YEARS

THE GAMES OF 1948-1960

CAROL PHILLIPS

"THE DIMPLED WORLD AND EUROPEAN CHAMPION MADE SPINS, SPIRALS and loops look like child's play as thousands of spectators in the stands and on snow-covered sun-bathed hills around the open-air Olympic Stadium shouted hoarsely, 'Barbeli, Barbeli!'"

Those were the words of Canadian Press reporter Jack Sullivan reporting from St. Moritz, Switzerland, the day 19-year-old Barbara Ann Scott of Ottawa won the 1948 women's figure skating gold medal.

Scott's victory was the highlight of the Games; not only for Canada, it seemed, but for the rest of the world, a world that was only just emerging from the ravages of war. The posh resort village of St. Moritz had been untouched by the war, and its abundance of hotels and restaurants had made it the site of choice for the International Olympic Committee.

But no matter how perfect a site may seem, there is always one factor you can never count on — Mother Nature. And in an era when both hockey and figure skating were held outdoors, the Canadian Olympic contingent was especially vulnerable to the weather's whims. By midday in St. Moritz, the sun often shone so brightly that the large ice surface melted into slush. The first day of competition for the women figure skaters was postponed after only two of five school figures had been completed. A combination of sleet, slush, and sun delayed competition the next day as well. Finally catching on, organizers decided to hold the competition first thing in the morning. The women laced up their boots and were on the ice at 7:30 A.M.

Barbara Ann Scott led throughout the event, but her victory took some fancy footwork and fast planning. The final free skate was slated for early afternoon, after a hockey game. The ice was to be flooded after the players left, causing a problem for the figure skaters in the form of shale ice, a thin layer of quick-frozen ice that develops over a pool of water. Scott and coach Sheldon Galbraith consulted. Down one side of the huge ice surface, there was a long narrow strip that had not been boarded off for hockey, where the ice would be better. They frantically reworked her program.

Cautious as she completed her first manoeuvres on the ice, Scott gained momentum in front of the biggest crowd since opening day. At the end of her program, she was swamped by photographers, reporters, and admirers even before her scores could be announced. Her coach ran interference as he guided her to the dressing room. Her mother, Mary, had to fight her way through the crowd, arriving just in time to see her daughter hoisted onto the shoulders of Canadian hockey players Reg Schroeter and Albert Renaud. The players, from the RCAF Flyers, Canada's best amateur team, were on their way to winning their own gold medal and regaining the supremacy lost to Great Britain in 1936.

A three-time recipient of the Lou Marsh Trophy for Canada's athlete of the year, Barbara Ann Scott was the most popular female sports figure of her generation. Her numerous credits included a 1947-48 world championship and a 1948 Olympic gold medal.

The RCAF Flyers restored Canada's hockey supremacy at the first Olympics to be held after the war.

At the start of the Games, it didn't look as if the hockey tournament was even going to get underway when two teams showed up representing the United States — one affiliated with the United States Olympic Committee, another sanctioned by the U.S. Amateur Hockey Association, member of the International Hockey Federation. The IHF threatened to pull the whole hockey tournament from the Olympics if its team was not allowed to play. Hockey was the big money-maker for the Games, so the Swiss organizing committee allowed the IHF team. But then the IOC overruled the local committee and banned both teams. Subsequently, it reversed its decision and allowed the IHF-sanctioned team to compete, but said the hockey tournament would not be official. Then it changed its mind again mid-way through the competition and announced the results would be official — except that all games against the United States would be exhibitions only. No matter, the United States lost to all three medallists, including a 12–3 loss to Canada.

The Canadian team, while remaining undefeated, wasn't exactly making friends during its tour of the Alps. In its first game against Great Britain, more animosity was felt towards the referees than between players. Some 21 penalties were given out, leaving both sides laughing and cracking jokes. But against Sweden, the game eventually broke into a brawl, and the Canadians were labelled unsportsmanlike.

The hockey games were consistently played on mushy ice. Sometimes they were postponed because of the terrible conditions. Canada was tied with Czechoslovakia for the lead heading into its final game against Switzerland. Both Canada and the Czechs were unbeaten. In the final game, against the Swiss, the Canadians were pelted by snowballs from the partisan crowd whenever the fans didn't agree with a referee's call. And the Canadian media grumbled that the officials were distinctly biased. Canada still beat the Swiss, 3–0, and won the gold medal by virtue of a better goal average.

Lost in all the hoopla of Scott and the hockey team was the bronze medal performance of pairs skaters Suzanne Morrow and Wally Diestelmeyer, who won in a blinding snowstorm. Their routine included the first performance ever of the death spiral with the woman's head touching the ice.

JEUX OLYMPIQUES D'HIVER
1948 S⸗ MORITZ SUISSE

The 1952 Winter Olympics were held in Oslo, Norway. Speed-skater Gordon Audley, a 23-year-old railway worker from Winnipeg, led the Canadian team into Bislett Stadium. Audley had been training on an ice-coated gravel pit along the Red River. "Before the race, I felt I'd be lucky if I got fifteenth or twentieth," he said after tying Norwegian Arne Johansen for the bronze medal in the 500-metre race.

Audley was paired with defending Norwegian champion Finn Helgesen. Audley fell behind about 10 metres into the start. He caught up at around the 110-metre mark and the two were neck-and-neck going into the stretch. Although they were clocked with the same time, Audley's spurt in the final five metres put him inches ahead of Helgesen, according to the judges. Appreciative Norwegian onlookers checked their stopwatches, then checked their programs to find out who this surprise Canadian was, before bursting into loud cheers.

In hockey, Canada was represented by the Edmonton Mercurys. Again, playing outdoors meant playing in adverse conditions. The team's second game, against Poland, took place in a blizzard. And again, the heavy body-checking brand of North American hockey drew boos from the crowd throughout the tournament.

The team's first challenge came from Sweden. In front of 10,000 screaming Scandinavians, the Canadians were down by two in the first period. Then they were tied at two apiece heading into the third. With twenty seconds left, centre Billy Gibson carried the puck behind the Swedish goal and passed to Billy Dawe, who was waiting outside the crease. Dawe deked the goalie and slid the puck into the net.

The team's next match against the United States also had last-minute heroics, but this time it was the Americans who celebrated. Canada had been up by two in the first period and were leading 3–2 with about two minutes left. In Jordal Stadium, packed with 10,000 fans who had stormed the gates in hopes of witnessing a rowdy, rough match, American Jimmy Sedin poked the puck past goalie Ralph Hansch and the game ended in a tie. Despite their reputation for hard play, the game between the two North American teams yielded only three penalties.

The tie gave Canada the gold medal and catapulted the United States from fourth to the silver medal position. Russian journalists charged that the tie game was fixed in order to prevent Communist Czechoslovakia from winning a medal (the results had left the Czechs in fourth).

Four years later, in an Alpine health and winter sports resort in northeastern Italy, the Soviet Union exploded onto the Winter Olympics scene. The U.S.S.R. won 16 medals, including seven gold, at the 1956 Winter Olympics at Cortina d'Ampezzo, more than any other nation. Canada, especially, would be affected by the new world sports power, right where it hurt —in hockey.

The first blow came when Canada, represented by the Kitchener-Waterloo Dutchmen, lost 4–1 to the United States in a steady snowfall. It was the first time a Canadian hockey team had lost since Great Britain won the gold in 1936 — and that had been the only loss to date.

The Soviets beat the United States to meet Canada in the final game. Canada needed to beat the Soviet Union by three goals to take the gold. The United States also needed the Soviets to lose. But the final score was Soviet Union 2, Canada 0. Canada had won the bronze, finishing behind the Russians and the Americans. It was bedlam at the end of the game. Russians threw their beaverskin hats in the air. Some ran into the crowd, grabbing and kissing the women. Russian fans cheered and jumped in unison. Other Russian players rushed onto the ice, shouting, kissing, singing, and even throwing their arms around Canadian players who had come to shake hands.

For Canadians, it was time for reflection and, of course, criticism. Canada should be sending an all-star team to the Olympics, argued James Dunn, president of the Canadian Amateur Hockey Association. Every other country sends an all-star team, he maintained. Coach Bobby Bauer backed up the suggestion "as an absolute necessity."

Canada's bronze performance in hockey fell short of expectations, and the same might be said for the second of three medals that Canada would win at Cortina d'Ampezzo.

Figure skating pairs team Frances Dafoe and Norris Bowden had been fifth in the 1952 Olympics and were entering the 1956 Olympic competition as two-time world champions. They had already decided that this would be their last year of amateur competition. The pairs' grand finale ended in controversy and disappointment. Although they skated cleanly throughout their performance, near the end the Canadians faltered on a lift and didn't finish on time with their music. A small mistake, but it was enough. Austrians Elisabeth Schwartz and Kurt Oppelt, who had finished second at the worlds, had four first-place votes and five second places. The Canadians had four first-place votes, four second places, and one third. The Hungarian judge had placed his own country's team ahead of both the Austrians and the Canadians. If they had received one more second-place vote, Dafoe and Bowden would have won the gold on point totals. Instead, they took silver.

"I guess we shouldn't be greedy," said Dafoe to reporters as she fought back tears. "We had our moment of glory. Now it's theirs."

World champion pairs skaters Frances Dafoe and Norris Bowden came within one vote of a gold medal in 1956, and had to settle for silver.

Alpine skier Lucile Wheeler, shown here in a 1958 race, was a bronze medallist at the Cortina d'Ampezzo Games.

There was one medal that Canadians could celebrate wholeheartedly. The ski team's trainer Josef Salvenmoser said at the beginning of the Games that the downhill course would suit St. Jovite, Quebec, native Lucile Wheeler, because it was similar to the giant slalom with a lot of gates at the top of the run.

Ironically, Wheeler, age 21, hadn't fared too well in the giant slalom and slalom races at these Olympics. She placed sixth in the giant slalom in the first days of competition, to give Canada its first point in the Games. But in the slalom she fell on her first run and was disqualified.

On the day after the hockey team had lost to the Russians, the Canadian team needed a pick-me-up, and Wheeler came through. On the steep first quarter-mile of the downhill course, she was clocked in first — right where Salvenmoser had said she was suited. She lost time when the course levelled out and she almost fell, but passed the finish line in third place for a bronze.

The 1960 Winter Games in Squaw Valley, California, opened amidst a snowstorm so fierce that the ceremonies had to be held during a lull in the weather. These were the much-celebrated Games when the U.S. hockey team won the gold — a victory not to be repeated for another 20 years. The Kitchener-Waterloo Dutchmen, after losing to the Americans, 2–1, beat the Russians 8–5 and won silver. But second wasn't good enough in the eyes of most Canadians. The Canadian team was again fiercely criticized back home.

Hockey aside, it didn't take Canada long to win its first gold of the 1960 Games. On the first day of competition, figure skating pairs team Barbara Wagner and Bob Paul, who had finished sixth in 1956, received first-place votes from every judge on the panel on their way to the top of the podium. It was the first time a North American pair had won the event.

In fourth place was a brother-and-sister team from Oakville, Ontario, Maria and Otto Jelinek, whose parents had escaped from Czechoslovakia when the skaters were just young children. The Jelineks would be future world champions for Canada.

A few days later, 19-year-old Canadian and North American champion Donald Jackson took centre stage as a prime hope to win a figure skating medal. He had finished second at the previous year's World's to American David Jenkins, and the Olympic competition looked to be a two-man battle for gold. But after the compulsory figures, Jenkins stood in second place, and Jackson, from Ottawa, was fourth. In the free skate, both men battled back. Jenkins won the gold and Jackson took bronze, the silver going to Czech skater Jarol Divin.

Ottawa skier Anne Heggtveit had an inauspicious start to the competition, finishing twelfth in both the downhill and the giant slalom. But on the second-to-last day of the Games, she made up for any disappointments she had ever suffered by winning the gold medal in the slalom.

"Beatings are tough to take," the 21-year-old told reporters. "I guess you've got to get hardened to them. I did, and today makes up for all those losses."

Heggtveit's roommate was a 16-year-old from Rossland, British Columbia, who had finished well back in all three ski events. Her name was Nancy Greene, and her time was yet to come.

Skiing was in Anne Heggtveit's blood; her father was a cross-country champion and her two uncles competed at the Olympics. In 1960 she became Canada's first Olympic skiing gold medallist.

OLYMPIC GAMES

29 JULY 1948 14 AUGUST
LONDON

That the 1948 London Summer Games took place at all was considered an achievement of Olympic proportions. The city was still devastated by the war. There was no money for a new stadium or housing for the athletes. But with some old-fashioned elbow grease, the existing facilities were spruced up and adapted for the Games.

Wembley Stadium was the principal site, hosting track and field. The Royal Air Force barracks were converted into housing for the athletes. Cynics said it couldn't be pulled off, but when the Opening Ceremonies got underway, there were 82,000 people at Wembley sweating in unison under the hot midday sun. The heat was punishing. Spectators collapsed and were carried out at a rate one per minute, according to reports. Still, the Canadian team marched in proudly, the men dressed in navy blazers and dark flannels and the women in blue blazers and white skirts.

Once the action began, the Canadian women's track team provided some exciting results. Viola Myers of Toronto and Pat Jones of New Westminster, British Columbia, finished fourth and fifth respectively in the 100-metre finals. Perhaps it was the London drizzle plaguing the day that caused the two sprinters to be less than excited about their performances. "I guess it's pretty thrilling to be in the first six," said the 21-year-old Myers. "But I am not impressed. I should have done better." "I am not very excited and certainly not satisfied with my showing at all," retorted Jones, 17.

They would have to wait until the final day of the track and field events to stand on the podium. That's when Myers and Jones teamed up with Dianne Foster of Vancouver and Nancy MacKay of Oshawa to win the bronze in the women's 4 × 100-metre relay in front of a crowd of 84,000.

The Canadian men's relay team came fourth that same day, after the U.S. team was disqualified for an illegal baton pass. Canada wouldn't see gold in this event for almost 50 years, when the glorious team of Esmie, Gilbert, Surin, and Bailey competed in Atlanta in 1996.

The next day, Canada could boast an Olympic record. Weightlifter John Stuart, from Verdun, Quebec, set the record in the press portion of the lightweight competition on his way to a fifth-place finish overall when combined with his snatch and jerk results. His teammate, Montrealer Gérald Gratton, finished fifth in the middleweight division — but his call to the podium would come in another four years.

At Henley-on-Thames, the Canadian canoeists raised the flag twice. Norm Lane, from Toronto, won the bronze in the 10,000-metre Canadian-type singles event, which has since been discontinued. He used a standard canoe, while the Czech gold medallist used a canoe that curved at the keel, allowing him to paddle on one side, instead of wasting energy maintaining a straight course. "I sometimes felt as though I was pushing a barge," said Lane after the race.

The next day, Doug Bennett, of St. Lambert, Quebec, battled both a crosswind and superior canoe used by another Czech gold medallist to win the silver in the 1,000-metre Canadian singles. He went on to finish fourth with teammate Harry Poulton in the doubles.

In yachting, Paul McLaughlin of Toronto had the best Canadian finish, placing fifth in the Finn class. He had been in first place heading into the second-to-last race of the series, but after colliding with the French entry during the race, he dropped to fourth overall. McLaughlin needed to finish first in the final race to have a shot at a medal. He finished seventh.

The 1952 Summer Olympics in Helsinki marked the debut of the team from the Soviet Union, after sending only "observers" in 1948. And thus was launched decades of U.S.–Soviet Union rivalry.

The Soviet Union team did not stay in the athletes' village. Instead, they were housed near a Soviet naval base under guard, surrounded by barbed wire, and with, reportedly, large portraits of Stalin hanging on the walls. No visitors were allowed.

A 17-year-old high school student from Saskatoon gave Canada its first summer gold medal since 1936. After finishing second at the world trap-shooting championships, George Genereux was asked what score he thought would win the Olympics. He said 192 (out of 200). And that's exactly what he shot. Described by Canadian Press reporter Alan Harvey as someone "who shoots as casually as a man flicks the ashes off his cigar," Genereux finished one point ahead of Swede Knut Holmqvist, who had needed a perfect final round to tie, but had missed his second-to-last shot.

It was a great opening weekend for Canada. While Genereux was shooting for gold, Gérald Gratton was in the midst of winning a weightlifting silver in the middleweight division. He equalled the Olympic record in the press portion of the

Olympic shooting today is divided into three categories, with a total of 11 events. Trap-shooter George Genereux took Canada's second-ever gold medal in shooting at the 1952 Summer Games.

competition, but ended up behind American Peter George, who set Olympic records in the snatch and jerk as well as overall.

On the lake, Kenneth Lane and Don Hawgood of Toronto won a silver in the 100-metre Canadian pairs canoeing competition. Former 10,000-metre silver medallist Norman Lane finished fifth this time around.

And on the track, Canada wound up a dismal meet on an uplifting note. The men's 4 × 400-metre relay team finished fourth behind a world-record-setting Jamaican team.

Later that week, Gilmour Boa of Toronto almost gave Canada its second shooting medal of the Games. At the end of the prone-position, small-bore rifle competition, Boa had been tied with an American, and a German was placed third. On further inspection of the inner rings of Boa's target, the judges dropped him to fourth.

Meanwhile, Canada's rowing team was making the best of a bad situation. In retrospect, they might have felt that their competition was over before it had begun. The team's double sculls and four- and eight-oared shells were being shipped from Montreal to Europe for the Games when the ship hit a hurricane in the North Atlantic, wrecking the boats beyond repair. Ironically, these boats were not the ones originally intended for racing at the Olympics. The oarsmen had had new boats made for them in Kelowna, British Columbia, but they hadn't arrived east in time for the sailing date and were still sitting at the Argonaut Rowing Club in Toronto. Unfortunately, there was no time to get these boats across the ocean. It was suggested the RCAF could help out, but when contacted by reporters, it declined.

And so just one week before the Olympics were to begin, a delegation left Helsinki for Stockholm to look over some Swedish-built shells that they could borrow. The only problem was that Europeans stroked from the port side while Canadians stroked from starboard. So either the boats would have to be converted to starboard rig or the Canadians would have to juggle their lineup.

After all that, none of the rowers qualified for the finals. Adding insult to injury, the four-oared crew without coxswain from the Hamilton Leander Boat Club placed third in its qualifying heat after one of its rowers caught a crab with his oar shortly after the start.

The Canadian team had Summer Olympic success in 1956 before the Melbourne Games even began. Due to Australian quarantine rules, the equestrian events had been held in June in Stockholm. The rest of the Games were to take place in November and December because of their location in the southern hemisphere.

Canada's team in the three-day equestrian event were Torontonians John Rumble, Brian Herbinson, and Jim Elder, riding Kilroy, Tara, and Colleen. The team finished seventh in the dressage portion of competition. Two days later the endurance trials were held on what was considered a severe and dangerous cross-country course, aggravated even more by overnight storms. It was muddy and slippery and ultimately some 68 horses fell, 20 riders were tossed, more than 10 riders had four or more faults, and several teams dropped out.

None of these disasters, however, included Canada, which came out with fewer jumping faults than any other country and catapulted from seventh to third overall. In the final show-jumping stage of competition, Canada held on for the bronze, finishing behind the powerhouses of Great Britain and Germany.

Like the equestrian event, these Games, for Canada, would focus on teamwork. And Canada's first medals came in rowing. The four-oared crew without coxswain came from the University of British Columbia — Don Arnold, I. Walter d'Hondt, Lorne Loomer, and Archie MacKinnon. They were actually the spares for the UBC

Canada's success in rowing is relatively recent. Our first rowing gold was won in 1956 by, left to right, Don Arnold, I. Walter d'Hondt, Lorne Loomer, and Archie MacKinnon.

Gerry Ouellette fired his way to a perfect 600 score and a gold medal in the 1956 prone-rifle event.

eights crew that was also competing and originally teamed up just to keep in shape. Only one of the four, Arnold, had previous rowing experience. The Canadian Olympic Association didn't want the expense of sending two crews, so Vancouver citizens took it upon themselves to see that both teams competed. The Vancouver Rowing Club set up a committee that took over the operation of training quarters. Food, linen, and laundry services were donated so that both the fours and the eights crew could concentrate on their training.

The novice fours crew won its first heat by five lengths. It won the semi-final by 12 lengths. And in the final, it won gold, beating the U.S. crew by five lengths, and earning Canada's first Olympic rowing title. The eights crew, meanwhile won silver, finishing less than a length behind the United States.

Canada's next two medals came in the prone-position, small-bore rifle competition. It may have been an individual event, but again teamwork won the day. Windsor tool designer Gerry Ouellette had done poorly in the three-position small-bore rifle event, while teammate Gil Boa of Toronto had shot a world record in the prone portion of the event on his way to placing a respectable sixth. So the two men decided to use Boa's rifle for the prone competition, meaning they would have to split its use within the same two-and-a-half-hour time limit. Boa shot first, coached by Ouellette. He scored 598 of a possible 600. Then Ouellette shot, coached by Boa. Sixty straight bull's-eyes later, he had a perfect 600 and the gold medal. Boa won bronze. Despite Ouellette's perfect score, it was not considered a world record because the targets had been set one and a half metres too close.

On the same day that Canadian shooters were making their mark on the competition, Hamilton native Irene MacDonald was heading into the springboard diving finals in second place and with her arm aching from bursitis. It became so painful that she balked on her second dive and was taken into the dressing room. Her retreat cost her six points and Canadian hopes looked dashed, but she returned with her left arm frozen by anaesthetic to complete her final four dives and hold on to the bronze medal.

The 1960 Summer Games in Rome went in the books as Canada's worst performance at the Olympics. The only medal was a silver, won by the eights rowing crew. The University of British Columbia team had rowed together for only four months, again funded by Vancouver citizens. Included in the crew was one rower from the 1956 eights silver-medal-winning team and three from the Olympic champion fours crew. They battled Germany throughout the entire race, pulling even, then falling back. In the end, UBC coach Frank Read blamed himself for missing gold by not keeping the rowers relaxed enough before racing.

In the pool, the men's 400-metre medley relay team placed fourth, anchored by Montreal native Richard Pound. He was the only Canadian to win points in two events that year — the relay and a sixth-place finish in the 100-metre freestyle. But his major mark on the Olympics would be made many years afterward, when he became president of the Canadian Olympic Association in from 1977 to 1982, and later an IOC vice-president.

No doubt the biggest heartbreak for Canada came with the ups and downs of sprinter Harry Jerome. In the Olympic trials, Jerome, 19, had run the 100 metres in 10 seconds flat. That matched the time run three weeks earlier by German Armin Hary. During international committee meetings held early in the Olympics, the two men were ratified as sharing the world record. So the duel was set between the Vancouver native and Hary heading into the sprint competition.

Disaster struck in the semi-final. Jerome was leading 40 yards from the finish when he suddenly pulled up and limped to the side of the track. Reporters found him in tears in the first aid room after being helped there by two other sprinters. The team masseur said it was a charleyhorse.

"I got it when I was really going," said Jerome to reporters. "I thought it would go away but, oh golly it kept hurting me, hurting me."

Armin Hary went on to win the gold. Jerome would have to wait another four years to get his second chance.

Barbara Ann Scott

GOLD MEDALLIST, FIGURE SKATING, 1948

When figure skater Barbara Ann Scott competed in Prague at the 1948 European Championships, her photograph appeared in the local newspapers 17 times in three days. When Rita Hayworth came to town just afterward, her photograph appeared only eight times. Such was the adoration and spotlight the 19-year-old from Ottawa lived under heading into the 1948 Winter Olympics.

"Glamorous" was often used to describe Scott. "Ice Queen" was how *Time* magazine referred to her when she was on its cover. She was constantly bombarded with questions regarding her professional plans, her love life, and rumours of a Hollywood contract. The comparisons with Sonja Henie, the most famous skater — and movie star — of them all, were constant. But Scott was also known as the skater who practised eight hours a day on her figures, and another one and a half hours on her free skate. It was once estimated she skated 11 miles a day on her figures alone. Such a regimen took her to the pinnacle: Canadian champion, North American champion, European champion, world champion, Olympic champion.

As a three-year-old, Barbara Ann Scott refused to wear the strap-on double-bladed skates that most children learn to skate on. Instead, she plunked herself down onto the bank of Ottawa's Dow Lake and demanded single-bladed skates with boots and picks. A year later, she asked Santa Claus for "real" skates. When her parents went to wake her Christmas morning, they found Scott sleeping with her new skates on — single blades with picks. She had crept down in the middle of the night and pulled them from under the tree.

Scott was a natural athlete. She learned to swim in two weeks. She climbed trees and hung by her knees from the branches. She rode horseback and played golf. When her father golfed the nine-hole course at Kingsmere, his "Tinker" (a nickname only her father used) caddied for him. Clyde Scott, a former lieutenant and prisoner of war, taught his daughter tenacity, as well as the neatness and precision necessary in figure skating.

By the age of nine, Scott was skating full-time at the Minto Club in Ottawa. At the age of 10, she became the youngest Canadian girl ever to pass the gold medal test, by passing the last of eight basic school figure tests. At 11, she was national junior champion.

Two years later in 1941, Clyde Scott, who had been working round the clock in his job at the Department of National Defence, collapsed while watching a bridge game and died. Heartbroken, Scott kept up her determination to succeed. At the age of 15, she became national senior champion.

Scott's major stumbling block was a shortage of funds to pay for skating instructors, skates, and competition expenses. Scott and her widowed mother, Mary, who chaperoned her daughter at all skating events, rented an apartment on the top floor of an old house and tried to stretch Mr. Scott's pension of about $3,000 a year. Friends came to the rescue and set out to raise the needed cash. Donations totalling $10,000 sent Scott to Davos, Switzerland, for the 1947 European Championships and then on to Stockholm, where she won the world championship.

When she returned victorious from Sweden, Scott was greeted by thousands of cheering fans who lined the streets of Ottawa as she was chauffeured in a cream-coloured Buick convertible to the Château Laurier Hotel. There the mayor presented her with the keys to another Buick convertible, canary yellow this time.

That gift set off a growl from Avery Brundage, president of the U.S. Olympic Committee. Despite the approval from the Canadian and American Amateur Athletic Union, Brundage declared that Scott had lost her amateur standing by accepting the car. She tearfully gave it back.

After winning the Olympics and world championships in 1948, Scott finally gave up her amateur standing to turn professional. No sooner had she made the announcement than her canary-yellow car was presented to her once again.

Its licence plate read 48-U-1.

After her phenomenally successful amateur career, Barbara Ann Scott skated professionally for five years. In her forties, she became a show-horse trainer and a top-rated equestrian.

CHAPTER FIVE

The OLYMPICS TRANSFORMED

THE GAMES OF 1964-1972

DOUGLAS HUNTER

From 1964 to 1972, over the course of six Games, winter and summer, the Olympic movement underwent a transformation at times exhilarating, at times traumatic. Amateur sport found an unprecedented international audience as the Olympic movement gained momentum in Third World nations, particularly African countries winning their independence from colonial rule. Cold War tensions between east and west heightened the stakes of sporting confrontations. Governments, democratically elected and otherwise, seized upon the Games' potential for championing their particular brands of ideology, turning high jumpers and bobsledders into foot soldiers in an international propaganda war.

In the postwar era, the Olympics as an ideological battleground found new momentum when the Soviet Union made its first Olympic appearance in 1952. In 1964, Germany participated as a unified team in an Olympic Games for the last time for three decades, the priorities of sporting goodwill only briefly overcoming the concrete barrier erected in Berlin.

American runners Tommie Smith and John Carlos extend gloved hands in a black power salute at the 1968 Mexico City Olympics, signalling the greater role played by politics and race in the Games.

Cannonades of boycotts, real and threatened, were fired back and forth. The International Olympic Committee banned Indonesia and North Korea from the 1964 Olympics for participating in the Games of the New Emerging Forces in 1963 in Jakarta, which had banned athletes from Israel and Taiwan. South Africa's apartheid policies got it banned from the 1964 Games; an attempt by the IOC to reinstate South Africa in 1968 was scuttled by a boycott threat from African nations. In 1972, the African nations again threatened a boycott over the participation of Rhodesian athletes under the British flag.

At that same Olympics, the People's Republic of China washed its hands of the Games over the participation of Formosa (Nationalist China), now Taiwan. Race as an axis of strife emerged most emphatically in Mexico City in 1968, when black American track athletes Tommie Smith and John Carlos, gold and bronze medallists in the 200 metres, stood on the medal podium barefoot with heads bowed and gloved fists extended while the American anthem played, their black-power gesture scandalizing the IOC even more than it did their own team.

Hundreds of international media representatives watch the action poolside at the 1972 Munich Games. The growing importance of television in promoting and financing the Olympics changed the face of the Games forever.

The Olympics were doomed to be exploited by *realpolitik*'s darkest impulses. The increasing politicization of the Games, in concert with their emergence as an international television spectacle, paved the way to the tragedy of the 1972 Munich Olympics, when 11 Israeli athletes were murdered by Palestinian terrorists. There was serious question of whether the Olympic movement could survive the deaths. It did, albeit shuddering through three successive boycotts in the process.

For Canada, this period represented an awakening to the allure of the Olympic stage. Individual brilliance began to be augmented by more concerted funding from the federal government. With Montreal securing the right in 1970 to host the 1976 Summer Olympics, nurturing sporting excellence became formal government policy; bureaucrats studying various national sports systems were most enamoured by the East German model and created a carding system to deliver financial support to amateur athletes.

But in 1956, when a Harvard MBA from London, Ontario, named Vic Emery saw a bobsled for the first time, being an Olympian was still very much a do-it-your-selfer's passion. Emery was living in Europe, and while cross-country skiing in St. Moritz, decided to pole over to the Winter Olympics in Cortina d'Ampezzo, Italy, to see what was going on. When he saw the bobsleds, he recognized his sporting future. At the time Canada had not a single bobsled run and certainly no Olympic bobsled team. Emery returned to St. Moritz the next winter to train with the British team, and while there he became hooked on the luge, the terrifyingly fast sledding discipline that would be named an Olympic sport in 1959. Emery introduced the luge to Canada in 1957 and was the first Canadian champion in the sport.

Emery had to wait eight years after his first exposure to the bobsled to make his Olympic mark. The 1960 Winter Olympics in Squaw Valley, California, were a cosy, village-style Games that had no room for either the luge or the bobsled, and the organizers were allowed to drop the events entirely. In 1964, Vic Emery, now a Montreal aircraft engineer, arrived at Innsbruck, Austria, for the Winter Games; with him in the four-man sled, *Canada 1*, were three other daredevil Canadian bachelors: Emery's

Canada plays the U.S.S.R. in 1964 at Innsbruck.

brother John, a plastic surgeon; Peter Kirby, a geologist; and Doug Anakin, a teacher. Though their own country scarcely understood the sport, this foursome was anything but an assemblage of Olympic "tourists" — athletes who were at the Games just for the thrill. In the opening two-man event, Vic Emery and Peter Kirby won the first heat and ended up just missing the bronze medal. In the four-man competition, guiding a sled designed by Italian Edwaldo d'Andrea, they set a blistering course record on their first run. They overcame a jammed rear axle after the second run with the help of the perennially selfless bobsledder Eugenio Monti. After the third run, Vic Emery had to be rushed to hospital when he had an adverse reaction to a tetanus shot. But he was back in command of the sled the next day for the fourth and final run. The ailing Emery brought it down the dizzying course with the third-fastest time, giving the Canadians a gold medal victory margin of exactly one second — an enormous gap in a sport in which hundredths of a second can separate winners and losers.

The Emery crew produced one of Canada's greatest Olympic achievements, yet

Members of Canada's colourful Olympic team congregate at the 1968 Winter Games in Grenoble.

the anonymity of their sport back home unfairly consigned it to the ranks of sporting trivia. Canadian hearts and minds were more attuned to the trials and tribulations of athletes in three other winter disciplines: hockey, figure skating, and alpine skiing.

Canada's unassailable supremacy in hockey had been dented in 1954, when the Soviet Union won its first world championship. An Olympic gold medal had followed for the Soviets in 1956, with Canada relegated to bronze, and in 1960 at Squaw Valley, an inspired American squad upset Canada 2–1 and went on to win gold. Following those Games, at which Canada had to settle for silver, our approach to international amateur hockey changed. In 1961, Toronto's St. Michael's College School suspended its Junior hockey program after its storied Majors won the national Junior title. The school's assistant principal, Father David Bauer, who was also the mastermind of its hockey program, felt that the school could no longer provide a proper education to the students playing a 60-game Junior A schedule. With the Majors program gone, Father Bauer set himself a new goal: a national team program based largely on collegiate talent, augmented by former professionals. Before Father Bauer, it had been Canada's custom to send a top Senior team to represent the country at a world championship or Olympic Games. In 1964 at Innsbruck, Father Bauer's charges played their hearts out and finished fourth. Although out of the medals, their inspired effort kept the program alive, and at the Games in Grenoble, France, in 1968, Canada was able to come away with the bronze.

In the eyes of many hockey enthusiasts, though, this was still a humiliation. Next to the North American professional game, international amateur hockey was viewed as a second-class sideshow; sportswriters routinely referred to Stanley Cup winners as "world champions," plainly believing that a match between a Soviet national team and a Stanley Cup-winning outfit like the Toronto Maple Leafs or Montreal Canadiens would be a fore-

Pairs skaters brother and sister Val and Sandra Bezic skated at Sapporo in 1972. Sandra Bezic later became a world renowned and highly sought after skating choreographer.

gone conclusion. And within the ranks of the Canadian amateur game, there was much resentment over having to play eastern bloc opponents like the Czechs and the Soviets, whom they viewed as "shamateurs."

In 1969, the Canadian Amateur Hockey Association, the federal government, and the National Hockey League joined forces to create a new entity, Hockey Canada, charged with restoring the glory of the maple leaf on international rinks. Hockey Canada received an important concession from the International Ice Hockey Federation: Canada would be allowed to use outright professionals when it hosted the world championships in 1970. Hockey Canada began signing new recruits to salaried contracts. But the Soviets were dismayed by the thought of facing Canadian professionals and through the IOC compelled the IIHF to withdraw the guarantee of professional eligibility for the 1970 worlds. Enraged, Canada pulled out of hosting the 1970 worlds and out of international amateur hockey. Canada did not participate in another Olympic hockey tournament until 1980.

Figure skater Karen Magnussen was 19 when she won Canada's only medal at Sapporo, a silver.

Canada's other winter sporting forte, figure skating, was fraught with its own complications. The 1960s produced some of the country's most glittering skating talent, moving the sport ahead both athletically and artistically. Yet that talent had to contend with the notoriously hidebound ways of judging, and team officials had to contend with the appeal to athletes of lucrative contracts with professional skating shows.

The years leading up to the 1964 Winter Olympics may have been the most outstanding in Canadian figure skating history. In 1962, siblings Otto and Maria Jelinek, fourth at Squaw Valley, won the world pairs title in Prague — a dramatic Cold War achievement, since the Jelineks' parents had defected from Czechoslovakia. Otto and Maria attended only after assurances were secured that they would not be detained the minute their feet touched Czech soil. At the same world championships, Donald Jackson, Olympic bronze medallist in 1960, won the men's single title with a dazzling performance that included the first triple lutz performed in competition. In 1963, 17-year-old Donald McPherson of Windsor, Ontario, became the youngest winner of the men's singles world title.

But the Canadian Olympic team was unable to capitalize on any of these successes as the professional figure skating circuit drew away its world champions.

Fortunately, the 1964 Olympic team had Petra Burka and pairs skaters Debbi Wilkes and Guy Revell. Fifteen-year-old Burka won the women's single bronze as Holland's Sjoukje Dijkstra swept the first-place votes. When Dijkstra retired from amateur competition after the Olympics, Burka moved up to win the 1965 world title. In pairs, Wilkes and Revell were able to extend Canada's pairs medal streak to five straight Olympics as they finished third behind a virtual dead-heat competition between the Soviet Union's Lyudmila Belousova and Oleg Protopopov, and Germany's Marika Kilius and Hans-Jürgen Bäumier. The Soviets edged out the Germans for the gold by eight-tenths of a point and two ordinals. After the Games, it was revealed that the German pair had signed professional contracts and performed in a revue before the Olympics ; they were stripped of their medals, turning the bronze of Wilkes and Revell into silver.

Professional skating only increased its allure for amateurs as the decade progressed. Before the 1968 Olympics, Burka joined the pros, and Canada found another amateur star: 15-year-old Karen Magnussen. The women's competition at Grenoble belonged entirely to American Peggy Fleming, who swept the first-place votes. Magnussen finished fourth in the free skate, but the scoring emphasis placed on compulsory figures left her in seventh.

Figure skating's modern age was on the horizon in 1968. At the 1968 Canadian team trials, an 18-year-old art student named Toller Cranston mesmerized the crowd and scandalized the judges with a flamboyant free skate. He was marked so poorly that he didn't even make the team. But Petra Burka's mother, Ellen, a leading coach, saw genius in Cranston and took him on.

The notoriously subjective sport was in one of its periodic episodes of aesthetic crisis as the skaters moved a step ahead of the judges and the marking system. In Sapporo, Japan, in 1972, Magnussen was magnificent in the free skate, but the emphasis on compulsory figures was so overwhelming that Austria's Beatrix Schuba, fifth in Grenoble and the defending world champion, was able to win the gold medal after finishing seventh in the free skate. Magnussen brought home a silver, Canada's only medal of the Games. Cranston, ninth in the men's competition, branded the judging a "joke." The Sapporo débâcle led to a downgrading of the importance of compulsory figures, and in 1973 Magnussen won the world title.

Alpine skiing had been added to the Olympic repertoire in 1948, and until Nancy Greene's performance in Innsbruck in 1964, the only Canadian athletes to have managed a top-eight finish at the Olympics in any of the alpine disciplines

were Lucile Wheeler, who won bronze in the 1956 downhill, and Anne Heggtveit, who took gold in the slalom in 1960. Hometown favourites, Austrians swept the medals in the women's downhill at Innsbruck, but Greene's seventh was noteworthy. She was the only North American to crack the top eight in the event, and Greene was only 20, with plenty of time ahead of her to move up into the medals. That, of course, she did in Grenoble in 1968, winning gold in the giant slalom and silver in the slalom, and becoming Canada's favourite female athlete for several years to come.

The hub of what would become known as the Crazy Canucks, a fearless group of men's downhill specialists who stole the international limelight in the 1970s, emerged on the national scene in 1968 in a 16-year-old named Jim Hunter. "Jungle Jim" skied in all three alpine events in Sapporo in 1972, and his finishes, while not top ten, were good enough to earn him an Alpine Combined bronze medal bestowed by the International Ski Federation. The next year, Ken Read, Dave Irwin, Dave Murray, and Steve Podborksi all joined the team.

Speed-skating was just beginning to find its legs in Canada. Government funding of the sport began in 1965, and in 1969 a future star emerged as Sylvia Burka of Winnipeg won the national women's junior title. Blind in one eye, she would inadvertently attract controversy in the Sapporo Games when she failed to see Anne Henning during a crossover and collided with the American star. Burka was disqualified, and Henning went on to win gold. Burka bounced back, enjoying a 15-year career that spanned three Olympics.

Silver winner in the slalom at Grenoble Nancy Greene (left) poses with her two French co-medallists. Greene also took gold in the giant slalom.

Harry Jerome (right) shakes the hand of silver medallist Enrique Figuerola after their 100 m win in Tokyo. Gold medallist and future Dallas Cowboy Bob Hayes is in the middle.

The Summer Olympics from 1964 to 1972 were a source of limited joy and numerous frustrations to Canadian athletes and their fans. The east-west geopolitical rivalry was turning the Games into a contest that left little room for the self-motivated, self-financed amateur. And while Canadian athletics came to adopt government funding and nationally managed coaching and competitive programs, medals proved consistently elusive. Canada won four medals in 1964, five in 1968, and five in 1972.

At the Tokyo Games in 1964, Vancouver's Harry Jerome was one of the greatest pure running talents ever seen, part of a fresh assault on the 100-metre event's unbroken 10-second barrier, which Jerome had run during the 1960 Olympic trials.

He was the only athlete to qualify for both Tokyo's 100- and 200-metre finals. Over the summer leading up to the Games, Jerome was moving at top speed. He ran 10.1 in the 100 metres in Oregon, and in August knocked off 200 metres in 20.4; at the time the world record was 20.2. In Tokyo Jerome had to settle for fourth in the 200-metre final, with a time of 20.8. After winning both his heats and his semi-final in the 100 metres, in the final he came up against American Bob Hayes, a future all-pro with the Dallas Cowboys. Jerome ran a very credible 10.2, but Hayes hadn't lost a race in 48 starts, and he matched Jerome's 10.0 world record and took gold. Hayes was seven feet ahead of Jerome and Cuban Enrique Figuerola at the finish, an unprecedented gap for an Olympic final, and Figuerola nosed out Jerome for the silver.

The 100-metre bronze in Tokyo proved to be Jerome's only Olympic medal, but his excellence exceeded the shorthand of Olympic roll calls. As other competitors came and went, Jerome kept running and kept recording first-class times. In 1968, eight years after matching the new world 100-metre record as a 19-year-old, Jerome competed in his third Olympic Games, in Mexico City, Mexico. In an extraordinarily close final, Jerome recorded a 10.1, only one-tenth of a second behind winner James Hines, and wound up seventh. Only two-tenths of a second separated the eight-man field.

Canada's one other note of track and field glory in these Olympic years came in 1964 in Tokyo, in the 800-metre final. Toronto's Bill Crothers was a certified long shot: the world record, set by defending Olympic champion Peter Snell of New Zealand, was 1:44.3, and Crothers's best time that season was 1:48.3, run in Montreal in June, four months before the Olympics. A gifted miler, Snell's specialty was 1,500 metres, and he decided to enter the 800 metres as well in Tokyo only at the last minute. Crothers made steady progress towards the final, recording 1:49.3 in his heat and 1:47.3 in the semi-final. In the final, Snell broke out of the pack after 350 metres to take the lead from Kenya's Wilson Kiprugut. Approaching the finish, the Kenyan stumbled on the heel of Jamaican George Kerr. He recovered, but not before Crothers had blazed past both him and Kerr, right on Snell's heels. Snell won with an Olympic record time of 1:45.1. Only half a second behind him, also under the old Olympic record, was Crothers.

It was out on the rowing course that Canada mustered the giant-killing performance of the Tokyo Olympics. George Hungerford had been bumped off the Vancouver-based eights shell when he came down with mononucleosis in the months leading up to the Games. As a consolation, he was allowed to put together a coxless pairs entry with fellow reserve team member Roger Jackson. They had never even been in a pairs race together when they showed up for the opening round of Olympic competition. The Canadian eight didn't make it to the Olympic final, but Hungerford and Jackson did, using a shell borrowed from the University of Washington team that

Swimmer Elaine Tanner came home from Mexico City as Canada's first female triple medallist— two silvers and a bronze.

had won gold for the United States in 1956. In the final, the Canadian pair rocketed to an early lead, then hung on grimly to edge out the Dutch crew by half a second to win Canada's only gold medal of the 1964 Games. Not a single Canadian reporter was on hand to watch them do it.

Canada began to emerge as a world power in the swimming pool at the 1964 Games. Although no medals were won, Canadian women distinguished themselves in several events. Marion Lay was fifth in the 100-metre freestyle, Jane Hughes fifth in the 400-metre freestyle, and Mary Stewart eighth in the 100-metre butterfly. Stewart and Lay, together with Patricia Thompson and Louise Kennedy, finished seventh in the 4 × 100-metre freestyle. The men's team also produced a finalist, Sandy Gilchrist, fifth in the 400-metre medley. Canada's fourth medal, a silver, was taken by Doug Rogers in the newly introduced judo event.

In 1968 in Mexico City, the swimming team provided Canada's finest moments of the Games. The team produced 19 finalists, a best-ever performance for a Canadian swimming team. Its stars included Ralph Hutton, the only athlete to reach three freestyle finals in the Games, winning silver in the 400 metres, and finishing fourth in the 200 metres and fifth in the 1,500 metres. Jim Shaw was fifth in the 100-metre backstroke. Sandy Gilchrist repeated the fifth place he had recorded in the 400-metre individual medley in Tokyo, and finished sixth in the 200-metre individual medley, one place behind fellow Canadian George Smith. In the 4 × 100 freestyle relay, Glen Finch combined with Smith, Hutton, and Gilchrist to finish seventh. Smith, Gilchrist, and Hutton teamed up with Ronald Jacks to finish fourth in the 4 × 200 freestyle relay; Shaw, Gilchrist, Bill Mahoney, and Toomas Arusoo were seventh in the 4 × 100 medley relay.

The women's team produced the most memorable Canadian athlete of the 1968 Olympics: Elaine Tanner, a 17-year-old Vancouverite who brought home three medals. Tanner won silver in the 100-metre and 200-metre backstroke, and with Angela Coughlan, Marilyn Corson, and Marion Lay, won bronze in the 4 × 100 freestyle.

And at the equestrian competition, the jumping team, led by Jim Elder astride The Immigrant, brought Canada its lone gold medal of the Games — and the last one until 1984.

Canadian swimmers had their work cut out for them matching their 1968 performances in Munich. World records crashed like panicked stock markets in a swimming war waged largely by Americans, Australians, and the emerging East Germans, and Canadian swimming finalists dropped from 19 to 10. Rare was a swimming event in Munich that didn't set a new world record. Canadian men came through with two medal-winning performances. Bruce Robertson took the silver medal in the 100-metre butterfly, swimming fast enough to have won gold in Mexico City; in Munich, he had to play second fiddle to the indomitable Mark Spitz. In the 4 × 100-metre freestyle relay, the men improved on their seventh in Mexico City with a fifth turned in by Robertson, Brian Phillips, Timothy Bach, and Robert Kasting. In the 4 × 200 freestyle, they dropped from fourth in Mexico City to seventh in Munich. The time posted by Robertson, Phillips, Ian MacKenzie, and Mexico City veteran Ralph Hutton was nearly 10 seconds better than the Canadian effort in Mexico City; the 1972 time would have won silver in 1968. In the 4 × 100 medley relay, Kasting, Robertson, Erik

Fish, and Bill Mahoney took the bronze with a time about two and a half seconds faster than the one that won the Americans gold in Mexico City. Swimmer Leslie Cliff won silver in the women's 400-metre medley and finished fifth in the 200-metre medley, while teammate Donna-Marie Gurr won bronze in the 200-metre backstroke.

Judo joined the Olympic roster of events in 1964; today there are seven events each for men and for women. Pictured above are members of Canada's 1972 Olympic judo team.

Canada's only medal of the 1972 Olympics to come outside the swimming pool was delivered in sailing, one of the least appreciated Olympic disciplines for Canadians, but one that had produced some of the country's consistently finest results. Since 1932, Canada had never failed to place at least one sailing competitor in the top eight, but a medal still eluded us.

That changed at Munich, when Dave Miller, John Ekels, and Paul Côté steered their Soling to third place in a 26-boat fleet, in a series shortened by light winds.

Canadian taxpayers invested approximately $2.5 million in their 1972 Olympic team, and there was general disappointment in the results, however unfair this was to individual athletes competing often unwittingly against eastern bloc athletes whose performances were illegally boosted by state-administered drug regimens. Apart from a cluster of silver and bronze in the pool and the sailing bronze, few Canadians got within hailing distance of a medal podium. There were some credible performances in track and field. Bruce Simpson came through with a fifth place in a pole

Bruce Simpson was a competitive pole vaulter for over 15 years. He placed fifth at Munich in 1972 and also competed at Montreal in 1976.

The Munich Olympics were the scene of the Games' worst tragedy, the slaughter of 11 Israeli athletes by Palestinian terrorists.

vault marred by bureaucratic bungling of approved pole construction materials. Abby Hoffman, a future president of Sport Canada, finished eighth in the women's 800 metres, as did Debbie Brill in the high jump. Other top-eight finishes included Donald Jackson's sixth in archery, Carroll Morgan's fifth in super-heavyweight boxing, Gord Bertie's sixth in flyweight freestyle wrestling and Doug Rogers's fifth in judo's open class.

The letdown the Canadian public experienced seeing gold medals adorning athletes from such smaller nations as Hungary and Bulgaria (which took home six each) was understandable, especially since Canada was preparing for an Olympic Games of its own in Montreal in 1976. In the battle of sporting superpowers, Canada was far back down the track in Munich, ranked twenty-seventh in medal winning. The country's escalating commitment to amateur sport funding wasn't producing anything close to an avalanche of medals and young athletes were finding it difficult to deal with their fellow citizens' exalted expectations.

Amateur sport had become a big business: for governments, sponsors, the media, and equipment manufacturers, and for some athletes as well.

Profile

Nancy Greene

GOLD AND SILVER MEDALLIST, ALPINE SKIING, 1968

There had never been anyone like Nancy Greene in Canadian athletics: a girl-next-door who excelled in a high-speed, high-profile sport, who won everything she could and then exited as gracefully from her discipline as any athlete could hope, a champion still adored by fans and respected by opponents. Other Canadian skiers, men and women, would win races and championships, but not with the same dominating presence as Greene, whose personality and achievements were pure gold.

Greene's ascent from casual club racer to international competitor was as good as overnight. At 14, she skied in her first Canadian junior championship in her home town of Rossland, British Columbia; at 16, she was wearing Canada's colours at the 1960 Olympics in Squaw Valley. She came by her talent naturally. Her parents went skiing on their honeymoon; her mother once competed in a national championship; her father helped build Rossland's first ski lift in 1946.

In Squaw Valley, the closest she came to a medal was the gold one slung around the neck of teammate and roommate Anne Heggtveit, won in the downhill. The medal's lustre captivated the teenaged Nancy. "I've never forgotten the experience of watching her stand up to receive her medal," Greene would recall in her autobiography, " and I resolved at that moment that I would one day win gold for myself — and for my country."

International competition as Greene found it verged on quaint, with more than a touch of élitism. She came to refer to the monopoly held by European racers as "the club." The Canadian team, for its part, was underfunded. At home in Rossland, the hat was passed to come up with $3,500 to send Greene and her coach, Verne Anderson, to Europe to

Nancy Greene retired from competitive skiing after her double medal win in 1968, her third time on an Olympic ski team. She was also World Cup champion in 1967 and 1968.

train with the national team over Christmas 1961. Training in Europe in the winter and on Canadian and South American glaciers in the summer, Greene progressed towards Innsbruck and the 1964 Olympics.

There, she produced a seventh in the downhill. Now 20, Greene began to blossom as a racer. Her emergence coincided with a more rigorous recruitment of Canadian team members, and with the debut of the World Cup tour, which quickly took over from the Olympics as the sport's competitive focal point.

Until the World Cup came along in 1966, skiing had had no annual world championship. It was left to the Olympics to choose the best every four years. The speed at which the World Cup was embraced as a major event rivalling the Olympics in importance took Greene by surprise. She was leading the nine-event World Cup in points in its second season, in 1967, when she returned home to help with national team fundraising and to promote the du Maurier race, Canada's first major international ski meet. Her absence from the tour for three races raised an outcry: how could she walk away from the tour when she was winning it? Rushing back to Europe after her obligations had been met at home, she won the last three races to secure the women's world title.

When the Olympics in Grenoble opened February 6, 1968, Greene was on her way to a second World Cup title and was the leading medal favourite among women skiers. But her Olympics opened with a disastrous tenth place in the downhill. As it had in half a dozen major races in her career, waxing had been her undoing. The soft wax selected for the downhill had picked up dirt, slowing her considerably. She called the race "the worst disappointment of my career."

She recovered immediately in the slalom. Fifth on the first run, she avoided the crashes and missed gates that plagued so many competitors on the second run to win the silver medal.

It was the giant slalom that provided her signal Olympic moment. Careful to avoid the waxing débâcle of the downhill, Greene prepared two sets of skis with the same wax. The first set she used for her practice run. The second set she carried to the start of the run that counted; when she put them on, the wax had never touched snow. Greene's gold medal victory margin of 2.64 seconds was unprecedented. The giant slalom gold and silver medals had been separated by one-tenth of a second in Squaw Valley, less than a second in Innsbruck.

Greene proceeded to win her second straight World Cup title, her final victory coming on her home mountain in Rossland. Appropriately, the Rossland World Cup was also Greene's last race. She retired, marrying national team coach Al Raine. As much as she had enjoyed her successes in Grenoble, she had sensed a disconcerting change in the Olympics. In Squaw Valley and Innsbruck, she had felt like a competitor. In Grenoble, where television dictated race scheduling and general event organization, she felt more like a performer. She left amateur skiing and the Olympics just as both were being transformed by professionalism and the imposing presence of the electronic audience.

CHAPTER SIX

MONTREAL'S EXTRAVAGENT GAMES

THE GAMES OF 1976

TRENT FRAYNE

I F THE TOPIC WERE CONFINED TO THE HEADY TRIUMPHS OF CANADA'S ATHLETES, there wouldn't be much to say about the 1976 Olympics.

Perhaps there were early unmistakable signs that 1976 was going to be a weird year for runners and jumpers and people who slide down mountains wearing barrel staves.

Innsbruck, Austria, twice provided a spectacular Alpine setting for the Winter Games, in 1964 and 1976. Kathy Kreiner (opposite) was only 14 when she joined Canada's World Cup team, 19 at the time of her 1976 Olympic gold medal win.

The city of Denver, a skier's paradise nestled high in the Rockies of Colorado, was awarded the Winter Games, but in a move without Olympic precedent, the state's voters ignored appeals and threats from government leaders, business tycoons, and editorial writers, and voted overwhelmingly to prohibit public funds from being used to support the Games' installations. So the Olympic oath was transferred to Innsbruck in the Austrian Alps, a town that only 12 years earlier had also staged the Games.

At Innsbruck, rhetoric, greed, and out-of-control spending were held to a minimum, not even a warm-up for what was brewing in Montreal, and dispatches from Austria were confined to the athletes. Many of them centred on the pursuit of Rosi Mittermaier, a West German ski star, who sought Olympic history in the three Alpine events, the downhill, the slalom, and the giant slalom. She had already won golds in the first two and now she was poised high above the treacherous 1,525-metre Axamer Lizum course seeking the third. She was scheduled fourth in the lineup of starters.

Ahead of Rosi, having drawn the number one starting post, was a tall slender blonde from Timmins, Ontario, Kathy Kreiner. Kathy had spent the winter on the World Cup circuit but had not had a good year. Two years earlier, she had won a World Cup giant slalom, but the well had been dry since. Indeed, she herself was not confident about her Olympic run. She had shipped her dress clothes home before the event, feeling she wouldn't require them for any post-race celebration.

The race was run in cloudy weather with occasional light snowfalls. The course was steep in parts and extremely demanding because mild temperatures had produced ice patches here and there. There was a drop of 385 metres from the start to the finish banner, and the downhill dive involved 49 gates.

At the starter's pistol, off went Kreiner, zigzagging seemingly with abandon down the mountainside, driving to the finish in 1:29.13, about a minute and a half of a daredevil descent. Three racers later it was Rosi Mittermaier's turn. After just over a kilometre, she was a half-second ahead of Kreiner's time. In the last half of the swift descent she encountered a split-second difficulty with one of the gates and the error cost her dearly. She zipped to the finish in 1:29.25, which translated into defeat by 12/100ths of a second. And so Kreiner was the world's best women's slalom skier that day, her triumph so unexpected that only one Canadian news reporter was on hand to watch the event.

Canadians had produced two medals prior to Kreiner's gold. In speed-skating, Cathy Priestner of Calgary was second in the 500 metres to Sheila Young of the United States, who already had earned a silver medal in the 1,500 metres and a bronze in the 1,000. The third medal, a bronze, arrived on the lonely vastness of the free-skating rink courtesy of Toller Cranston.

With only three medals at Innsbruck to stir them, Canada's sports followers looked ahead to the Summer Games in Montreal for taller rewards. But what greeted them as the months rolled towards the July Opening Ceremonies was a shocking, hilarious, inept, and virtually unbelievable preamble. It was the first time

Toller Cranston's skating artistry was slow to gain Olympic approval, but he did win a bronze in 1976. Right: Cathy Priestner earned six national speed-skating titles over her career, in addition to her 1976 Olympic silver medal.

the Summer Games had been staged on Canadian soil, and the opportunity soon produced the largest pork barrel in Canadian history.

Canada had outmanoeuvred Moscow and Los Angeles for the Games, owing to the persuasiveness and tenacity of Montreal mayor Jean Drapeau, who had talked glowingly of a return to the old values of a modest Games in the spirit of modern founder Pierre de Coubertin. Somewhere in the intervening six years, a grandiose fantasy took hold and Drapeau decided that the structures of the Games should be lasting monuments. To achieve his dream, the mayor countenanced no cost as being too great. Budgets went out the window. Criticism piled upon criticism, but the mayor paid no heed. Responding to charges that Olympic spending and planning had reached extravagant proportions and could be better spent providing sorely needed low-cost housing in the poor sections of Montreal, the mayor blithely told a Board of Trade audience that "2,500 years ago Pericles too was criticized for building the Acropolis instead of warships."

Drapeau declared repeatedly that the Games would not cost the taxpayers a cent (two decades later they were still paying for them), and at one point when the projected cost of the Games was set at $124 million he observed that there was no more chance that the installations would exceed the budget "than of my having a baby."

As the Games approached, their monstrous cost far overshadowed any other topic. Nick Auf der Maur, a Montreal city councillor and later a columnist for the *Gazette*, brought out a book, *The Billion-Dollar Games*, soon after the Olympic flame was extinguished. It documented the bungling and greed of Olympic construction, a story of incompetence, duplicity, nepotism, and corruption that caused the cost of the Games to soar to $1.5 billion. Auf der Maur wrote that lack of controls and unscrupulous contractors with open-ended contracts sent costs out of sight. Also, the unions took advantage of power struggles inside the organizing committee to make outrageous demands, and they got their way because the date of the Opening Ceremonies was inflexible and drawing ever closer. The prima donna Parisian architect Roger Taillibert, lured by Drapeau, was slated to get a fee greater than the combined fees of all the architects in Quebec for the previous year.

The three major networks in the United States began preparing their bids for the 1976 television rights soon after the Games ended in Munich in 1972. NBC and CBS,

Montreal mayor Jean Drapeau staked his career on the success of the extravagant 1976 Summer Games, which embodied his *politique de grandeur*. In spite of their inflated cost and rampant corruption, Drapeau was re-elected in 1978.

waiting for bids to open, were astonished in November of that year to learn that the Montreal Organizing Committee, called COJO, had signed a secret deal with the American Broadcasting Company that provisionally gave ABC the U.S. rights for $25 million. This was an Olympic record, almost twice the Munich amount of $13 mil-

lion. In addition, ABC got the right to match or top any higher bid from the other two big American networks. But it wasn't the terms of the agreement that outraged ABC's competitors as much as the fact that the deal was made secretly without their getting a chance to bid.

As is often the case, international politics took centre stage even before Montreal's Opening Ceremonies could take place. Belatedly, the Department of External Affairs in Ottawa became aware that the athletes from Taiwan planned to march under the

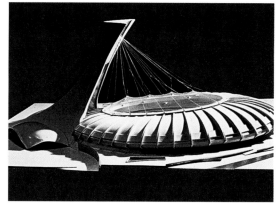

The Big O, Montreal's Olympic Stadium, has become a local landmark.

flag of the Republic of China. Five years earlier the Canadian government had switched its diplomatic recognition from the Republic of China in Taiwan to the mainland People's Republic of China. Ottawa recognized only Peking (it wasn't called Beijing back then). Accordingly, applying diplomatic house rules, the federal government decreed that Taiwan's athletes would not be permitted to land in Canada if they insisted on marching under their own flag.

Taiwan held firm and so did Ottawa. And, backing Taiwan, so did the IOC under its leader, the gruff, beefy, red-faced Irishman, Lord Killanin. Adding fuel to the controversy, the United States government recognized Taiwan, and its delegation presented the veiled threat that if Taiwan were not recognized, the U.S. might withdraw its athletes. Lord Killanin finally came up with a compromise solution: the Taiwanese athletes would march under the five-ring flag of the IOC. Later he told the media that IOC members had voiced "unanimous condemnation" of the Canadian government's interference.

The political wrangling did not even end with the Taiwan controversy. Next, 28 African nations threatened to leave Montreal, using the Olympic spotlight to protest a tour of South Africa, the land of apartheid, by the famed New Zealand rugby team, the All-Blacks. Rugby wasn't an Olympic sport, but the threat was real enough, because the 28 nations insisted that New Zealand's Olympic athletes be banned from the Games as a symbol of protest of the rugby tour (the All-Blacks, incidentally, were all white; the name in part described their uniforms). The IOC declined the threat and the African athletes were shipped home by their political bosses.

Finally, though, the great moment came: opening day in the vast new stadium, and notwithstanding all the acrimony and politicking and grotesque expense, it was a wonderful moment. Some 8,000 young athletes paraded in front of 70,000 enthralled spectators. Even before the Canadian athletes came marching into open view, the crowd on the far side of the stadium could see them, and they set up a roar of welcome that just swelled and swelled as the young men and women marching behind sprinter Abby Hoffman, the flag-bearer, started down the brick-red running track past the royal box. There, Elizabeth II, a solemn figure in a shrimp-pink suit and a draped turban to match, stood with her hands clasped in front of her, and when Hoffman dipped that Canadian flag and the hundreds of Canadian athletes snapped their eyes right, there was an absolute din of sound, an enormous wave of cheers as people stood, banging their hands together and yelling themselves hoarse.

On the first day of competition, Canada earned its first medal. In the Olympic pool, East German women set a world record in the 4 × 100 metre medley relay, the Americans close in their wake, and just a finger tip behind them the Canadian foursome of Wendy Hogg, Robin Corsiglia, Susan Sloan, and Anne Jardin earned a bronze medal.

Women's swimming provided the bulk of the medals for Canada in Montreal, one silver and six bronzes.

In subsequent days, though, Canadians found the medal podium a difficult step to climb. Indeed, for the first time in Olympic history, the host country failed to lay claim to a single gold medal. Overall, Canadians won five silver medals and six bronze. Nancy Garapick was the lone home-country performer to pick off two

medals — bronze rewards as a back-stroker in the 100 and 200 metres. In the 400-metre individual swimming medley, Canadian women won two medals in the one event — Cheryl Gibson the silver and Becky Smith the bronze. Shannon Smith won an individual bronze in the 400-metre freestyle. Relay star Anne Jardin added a second bronze to her collection,

The medley relay team won the sole men's swimming medal, a silver, in 1976.

anchoring the third-place 100-metre freestyle quartet that included Gail Amundrud, Barbara Clark, and Becky Smith.

Canada's men couldn't win for losing, until the relay team in the 4 × 100 medley splashed to a silver medal. Steve Pickell, Graham Smith, Clay Evans, and Gary MacDonald did it, chasing the American entry to a world's record. Then John Wood, the home country's premier paddler, thrilled a crowd of 5,000 lining the course when he led from the start of the 500-metre canoe sprint until the final strokes. Right at the finish, he was nipped by the race favourite, Aleksandr Rogov. Meantime, an unexpected silver was contributed when equestrian Michel Vaillancourt, riding the jumper Branch County, became the first Canadian in history to ride an individual Grand Prix jumping competition. The West German Alwin Schockemöhle won the gold with a fault-free ride.

Michel Vaillancourt's silver-winning jumper, Branch County, was a converted race horse.

113

The pursuit of a gold medal in track and field came down to high jumper Greg Joy. The Vancouverite was still in contention when it came to the final jump, but his dream was dashed when he knocked the bar from its moorings, earning a silver behind Polish jumper Jacek Wszola.

High jumper Greg Joy made his silver-winning jump in a downpour of Olympian proportions.

While Joy's silver was a surprise, most of Canada's pre-Games stars couldn't get out of the starting gate. Debbie Brill, the fourth-ranked high jumper in the world in 1975, a young woman who came within a whisper of clearing six feet three inches in the Olympic trials in Quebec City just a month earlier, went out in the preliminary jump at only five feet nine inches. While Pentathlete Diane Jones was sixth in her event, pole-vaulter Bruce Simpson, fifth at 17 feet at Munich in 1972, fell far short of that figure.

With few Canadian medals to write about, journalists were forced to focus on other issues. First, they banished a sprinter, Bob Martin, from the Canadian team and removed his village credentials. His crime: sneaking a friend into the village and providing him with room and board. Next, on the eve of the Closing Ceremonies, seven more Canadian athletes, all swimmers, were expelled from the village by the ever-alert officials. The

Mounties added local colour for tourists at the Montreal Games.

swimmers, ranging in age from 14 to 23, their events long completed, had left the village for a view of night life in wicked old Montreal. They missed curfew and, worse, they missed practice the following morning.

Canada's athletes won no golds on the fields of play, making Montreal's Games a first in that category. All other hosts captured golds at Games on their turf.

Profile

Kathy Kreiner

GOLD MEDALLIST, GIANT SLALOM, 1976

In the eight-year span from 1968 to 1976, three determined young Canadians sped down European mountainsides as swiftly and fearlessly as anyone in the women's skiing universe — and often reached the bottom faster.

Particularly in the twisting challenge of the giant slalom, these Canadians were dangerous opponents. Rushing through an Alps descent near Grenoble, France, at the 1968 Winter Olympics, freckle-faced Nancy Greene of Rossland, British Columbia, far outsped an assortment of starry women from Austria, Switzerland, and France to win a gold medal in the giant slalom's rugged crucible. Four years later, on the side of a mountain near Sapporo, Japan, Laurie Kreiner of Timmins, Ontario, missed a bronze medal by a mere 13/100ths of a second in the 1972 Olympics, trailing the gold medallist, Marie-Thérèse Nadig of Switzerland, by less than three seconds in a race that consumes about a minute and a half of mountain-sliding.

In 1976, the Kreiner family was back again. This time it was Laurie Kreiner's sister, Kathy, youngest in a family of six children. For a lot of Europeans, Kathy Kreiner performed the unforgivable on that cloudy afternoon on the treacherous Austrian slopes: she deprived the people's choice, Rosi Mittermaier of next-door Germany, of an unprecedented triple gold triumph. Mittermaier had won European hearts with victories in two earlier Alpine events, the slalom and the downhill, so she required only the giant slalom, the GS as ski fans call it, to complete the triple.

Kathy Kreiner was not the skier expected to upset Rosi, if anyone did. The fair-haired 18-year-old from Timmins, Ontario, had made a brilliant debut on the World Cup circuit as a child of 16 when she won at Pfronten, Germany, in 1974, but she had been blanked since then. Undaunted, Kreiner had spent the summer of 1975 working hard on her conditioning. With sister Laurie, she did pushups and situps and ran on country roads to hone muscles, while their mother went along to time their runs, carry equipment for weight training, and lend untiring encouragement.

Reaching Innsbruck in February, Kreiner felt ready and even buoyant, and the feeling persisted despite a sixteenth-place showing in the downhill. But slalom racing was her forte. Kreiner had the physique for the twisting, turning nature of slalom descent — she was a lithe five foot seven inches and 130 pounds and had a trim body apart from the powerful thighs of all successful alpine racers. Even so, in the slalom event that preceded the giant slalom, she missed one of the gates and had been disqualified.

Still, on the day of the GS she approached the start with confidence. As she rode the chair-lift towards the starting hut, she zeroed her mind on the 49 gates she would have to swerve past. At the summit she gave no thought to Rosi Mittermaier or any of the 41 other skiers reaching for medals, even sister Laurie.

The skies were low, wall-to-wall cloud, and there was occasional light snow. Then, leading the large field, Kreiner was off, hopping into high gear and whooshing down the long and occasionally icy route. She didn't let the course dictate to her. She attacked it, crouching low to swerve in and out of the flag-marked descent. She brought everything she knew about skiing into her plunge for a 1:29.13 drive.

Then she waited while the long trail of skiers strove to outrush her, including the fourth one down, Rosi Mittermaier. Mittermaier led over the course in a driving, attacking run, and at the halfway point had caught Kreiner's time and even surpassed it by a fraction of a second. But through the second part, she had a moment's difficulty with a flag. She hesitated almost imperceptibly, but enough to miss catching Kreiner's time by the mere blink of the eye.

At the top of the course, Laurie Kreiner revelled in her sibling's first-place standing while skier upon skier pushed off and failed to match it. With victory for Kathy assured, Laurie skied the course in tears of joy, unplaced, and continued right into her sister's arms amid the throng beyond the finish line.

In the months and years that followed, nothing in skiing matched this shining moment for Kreiner. Indeed, coaches frequently shifted her from GS to the downhill. She had hoped she might be chosen to carry Canada's flag at the Opening Ceremonies of Lake Placid's 1980 Winter Games, but the Canadian committee fingered skier Ken Read. She hoped for a similar honour at the Montreal Games, but the chosen athlete was veteran distance runner Abby Hoffman.

In June of 1981, Kathy retired from World Cup skiing. She accepted an athletic scholarship at the University of Utah. And there, on American soil far from the homeland upon which she had bestowed its only gold medal five years earlier, Kathy Kreiner began showing American young women how she did it.

Downhiller Kathy Kreiner upset European favourite Rosi Mittermaier with her gold medal-winning 1976 giant slalom run.

CHAPTER SEVEN

CANADA'S GOLD RUSH

THE GAMES OF 1980-1984

DEREK FINKLE

ONLY SIX WEEKS BEFORE THE OPENING CEREMONIES OF THE 1980 OLYMPIC Winter Games in Lake Placid, New York, the decade of yuppies, music videos, and personal computers was ushered in as the Cold War heaved one last painful gasp before expiring. U.S. president Jimmy Carter was piecing together a new foreign policy that would let the world know just how perturbed his government was with the Soviet Union's invasion of Afghanistan. Along with the usual options of economic, cultural, and diplomatic sanctions, Carter tossed his eye-opening trump card on the table — an American boycott of the Moscow Olympics later that summer. And not only would the American team be absent, Carter would do his best to convince as many nations as possible to stay away. Canadian prime minister Joe Clark's phone number was sure to be near the top of Carter's list.

Carter was well aware that an American-led boycott in 1980 would have more profound implications than the one briefly contemplated against Hitler's Berlin Olympics in 1936. It was estimated that the Soviet government had invested billions of dollars in preparing for the Moscow Games. The Americans represented the largest buyer of TV rights, planning to spend more than $100 million. When Carter asked the U.S. ambassador to Moscow which tactic would have the most punitive effect on the Soviets — an Olympic boycott or trade sanctions — the ambassador replied, "There's no question. The Olympics would." With that in mind, Carter started to make headway, locating sympathetic ears in Canada, Great Britain, China, Australia, New Zealand, the Netherlands, and West Germany. Towards the end of January, Carter announced that, barring the withdrawal of Soviet troops from Afghanistan by February 20, his country's best athletes would be spending the summer at home.

Canada's 1980 all-amateur hockey team failed to make medal-round play.

This ultimatum hovered over the small town of Lake Placid (population 2,731) like a high-pressure system as the Winter Games got under way on February 13, 1980. Almost 50 years earlier, Lake Placid had been a fashionable New York ski resort when it was chosen to host the 1932 Olympics. The decision to return to what had become, a half-century later, a worn-out town with 20 per cent seasonal unemployment rates, was beginning to look like a mistake of infamous proportions. Before the Olympic torch had even been lit, stories of local real estate scams, disastrous transportation planning, and the cinder-block Olympic Village (designed to be turned into

a federal prison after the Games) had garnered international attention.

For a northern nation, Canada had been an underachiever at winter Games, winning only eleven gold medals — five of them at hockey — since 1924. And things weren't looking any more promising for Lake Placid. From our 59-member team, including the 20-man hockey squad, our best hope for gold lay with the men's downhill ski team. Ken Read, who was in the number two position in World Cup standings, led fellow Crazy Canucks Steve Podborski, Dave Irwin, and Dave Murray on the slopes. On the women's team, 1976 giant slalom gold-medallist Kathy Kreiner was being joined by 19-year-old Laurie Graham, who had started to show great promise. The young ski-jumping contingent of Horst Bulau, Tauno Kayhko, and Steve Collins had been upstaging veteran jumpers lately and, together, they were considered an unpredictable talent, Canada's dark horse.

With professional hockey leagues across North America in full swing in February, Canada had not competed in Olympic hockey since 1968, when Father David Bauer's amateur squad won a bronze medal. So who, you might ask, resurrected a team in 1980? Father David Bauer. Considered by most to be an experiment, the quick young Canadian team, composed entirely of amateurs, was grouped with the U.S.S.R., a

Horst Bulau was a member of the 1980 and 1984 Olympic ski teams; in 1979 he had become Canada's first world-level gold medallist when he won the 70 m world junior title.

perennial hockey power. Bauer let it be known that his team's real, more attainable goal was defeating Finland, not the Soviets. Father Bauer's team struggled more than they should have in their opening games against Holland and Poland and, in the third round, the one they had been gearing up for against Finland, they gave what most considered an uninspired performance and lost 4–3.

On the day after the Opening Ceremonies, Ken Read pushed his way through the starting gate at the top of Whiteface Mountain's downhill course. Fifteen seconds later, his race abruptly ended when one of his bindings separated from his ski boot during the third turn. While Dave Irwin was pleased with his eleventh-place showing, Steve Podborski pulled through for his teammates and country, skiing an excellent race, good enough for a bronze medal. Podborski's bronze would be the only medal bestowed on Canada for an alpine event. Kathy Kreiner clocked a personal-best time in the women's downhill, but it earned her only fifth place. Laurie Graham missed the top ten by 3/100ths of a second. In ski jumping, our trio of teenagers misplaced their wings in the 70-metre event, but at 90 metres, 15-year-old, five-foot-three, 105-pound Steve Collins placed ninth.

On skates, Canada was slightly more impressive. It was a weak year for figure skat-

American speed-skater Eric Heiden, with five gold medals at Lake Placid, provided fierce competition for Quebec's Gaëtan Boucher, who won silver in the 1,000 m.

ing, and the best showing was from the dance pair of Lorna Wighton and John Dowding, who were consistent with their pre-Games ranking of sixth. Although their strongest work was yet to come in the years ahead, pairs skaters Paul Martini and Barbara Underhill finished ninth. Fourteen-year speed-skating veteran Sylvia Burka, who was competing in her third Winter Olympics, announced that she was retiring from the sport after coming tenth in her favourite event, the 1,500 metres, and seventh in the 1,000 metres.

The undisputed Canadian star of the thirteenth Winter Games was 21-year-old speed-skater Gaëtan Boucher from Ste.-Foy, Quebec. Aside from winning a silver medal, Boucher's profile was boosted by coming second to the man who was the individual standout of the entire Games, Eric Heiden. The amiable American won an unprecedented five gold medals, setting Olympic records in his first four races and a world record in his fifth. Even though Boucher finished eighth in the 500 metres, Heiden was happy to see the explosive Canadian at his side for the start of the 1,000 metres. "Gaëtan has a great start, a good 600 metres, and I can look over at him and know where I stand against the rest of the world."

Along with Heiden's exploits on the speed-skating track, the American audience was captivated by the Cinderella story of their gold medal-winning hockey team (a first since 1960), which included an unbelievable 4–3 victory over the powerhouse "amateur" Soviet team. To this day that game is referred to by the American media as "The Miracle on Ice."

Despite the hundreds of spectators wearing "NOLYMPICS" and "Let the Soviets Play With Themselves" T-shirts, President Carter's February 20 deadline came and went, passing by as just another day at the Olympics, and Soviet troops were still in Afghanistan when the Lake Placid Games came to a close four days later.

While it was still unclear how the Canadian government was going to vote on the boycott issue, the Canadian Olympic Association convened on March 31 and voted against the idea 25 to 5. The crucial section of its four-point resolution stated: "The COA rejects in principle the concept that Canadian Olympic athletes bear the burden of Canada's response to an international situation."

However, the COA was unable to stop the growing support for a boycott. Through External Affairs Minister Mark MacGuigan, Pierre Trudeau's newly elected Liberal government informed a practically empty House of Commons: "This government believes that the international situation brought about by Soviet aggression in Afghanistan makes it wholly inappropriate to hold the Olympics in Moscow."

COA president Dick Pound was outraged. He accused Trudeau's government of "Mickey Mouse" politics, calling the boycott "the most flagrant use of the Games for political purposes that has occurred in modern times." Still, other Canadian institutions fell quickly into line with the government's decision. The day after MacGuigan's announcement, for example, the CBC elected to cancel its radio and TV coverage, writing off the $2.4 million it had already paid in advance for coverage rights and rental of facilities.

Canada's decision to stay away from Moscow was made official in late April when the COA voted 137–35 in favour of the boycott. The U.S. State Department could thus announce that 60 nations, including Canada, would pass up the Moscow Games. The Soviet government was understandably bitter at seeing its monumental preparations and efforts ignored by a significant and wealthy portion of the world. "The Americans don't like us," the Kremlin said, and that became the official Soviet line throughout the much reduced Moscow Games.

If 1980 had been a less-than-stellar year for Canadian Olympians, the country felt buoyed with hope four years later for the Winter Games in Sarajevo, Yugoslavia, when everyone hyped the national team as potentially the best ever. Barbara Underhill and Paul Martini ranked among the top three skating pairs in the world, and Brian Orser of Orillia, Ontario, entered the Games as the four-time Canadian men's skating champion. Things looked a little more dicey in men's downhill skiing with Ken Read retired and reckless young Todd Brooker on the injury list, but Steve Podborski, based on a win in the 1982 world championships, had the promise to beat his bronze medal at Lake Placid. On the women's side, the focus was on the comeback of Gerry Sorensen, a seasoned veteran at 25. A terrible injury in 1978 had cost her a year on the slopes, but post-1980, she had registered four World Cup victories, and at Sarajevo, she led a strong team that included Laurie Graham, Karen Stemmle, and Diana

The 1984 Winter Games in Sarajevo marked the last major international event in the city before it succumbed to the brutality of civil war.

Haight. As for the trio of teenage ski-jumpers who represented Canada at Lake Placid, Horst Bulau had emerged as the dominant figure, third in World Cup standings in both 1981 and 1982, and the hope was that he'd break through at the '84 Games.

Once again, the Soviet Union's hockey team, featuring the legendary goaltender Vladislav Tretiak in his swan song Olympiad, was loaded with enough talent that, barring another "Miracle on Ice," made it a lock for the gold. With the Czechoslovakians expected to take silver, it looked as though Canada and the United States would battle it out for the bronze. Knowing that Canada was going to be their last obstacle to a medal, U.S. Olympic officials challenged the amateur status of four Canadian players who had signed contracts with teams in the National Hockey League. Alan Eagleson, Canada's international hockey guru, declared that only two of the players in question, Mark Morrison and Don Dietrich, had suited up to play in the NHL, and that because they had played 10 games or less they were still eligible, according to the International Ice Hockey Federation. Eagleson was also quick to point out that two members of America's celebrated 1980 squad had signed professional contracts before Lake Placid.

After protests by both the Americans and Finns, the International Olympic Committee ruled that any hockey player who had played one solitary shift for a professional hockey team was ineligible for the Olympic Games. Hours before Canada's opening game with the United States, the team lost the services of forward Mark

Morrison and defenceman Don Dietrich. It was a controversial decision, one that didn't seem to apply to Toronto-born Richard Cunningham of the Austrian team, who had played more than 300 games in the World Hockey Association before the league had folded. Still, Canada defeated the United States 4–2 and then Austria 8–1 before advancing to the medal round with a 4–2 victory over Finland.

With the phenomenal American speed-skater Eric Heiden well into retirement, Gaëtan Boucher was expected to eclipse his silver performance in 1980 with a chance to garner medals in a number of races. Considering that Boucher had fractured his left ankle in three places while training in Montreal less than a year earlier, his return to the top of his field was remarkable. Despite facing stiff competition from Japan and the Soviet Union, the man from Ste.-Foy, Quebec, who toiled at what was considered a fringe sport by the vast majority of his fellow Canadians, was counted on to become, for two weeks anyway, a national treasure.

While Sarajevo avoided the organizational problems that had plagued the Lake Placid Games, the biggest worry was the lack of snow. Fortunately, after three days of competition, the city, nestled in the picturesque Zvijezda Mountains, was covered in a blanket of snow thick enough to briefly bring the Games to a halt. But by the time the roads had been ploughed, Gaëtan Boucher was Canada's only medal winner with a surprising third-place finish in the 500 metres. Days later he followed this achievement with golds in both the 1,000- and 1,500-metre races, becoming the first Canadian in Olympic history to win more than two individual Winter Games gold medals.

The highly touted figure skating pair of Underhill and Martini, in their final amateur competition, were not at their best. Skating to the music of Benny Goodman's "Sing, Sing, Sing" in the pairs short

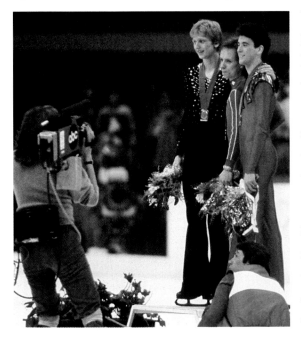

At Sarajevo, Gaëtan Boucher became the first Canadian winter games triple medallist. Left: Silver medallist Brian Orser shares the podium with American skater Scott Hamilton (gold) and Czech skater Jozef Sabovtchik (bronze).

125

The combination of show business and Uncle Sam made the 1984 Los Angeles Summer Games an exciting extravaganza. The Soviet-inspired boycott greatly boosted Canada's medal wins, which totalled 44. Right: Swimmer Alex Baumann captured gold in both the 200 m and the 400 m individual medleys.

program, Underhill lost her balance during one of the easier required moves, a sit spin, and the couple placed sixth. After the free-skating program, they dropped a notch and wound up a disappointing seventh.

Like Underhill and Martini, Brian Orser also got off to a shaky start, coming seventh in the compulsory figures section of the men's program. But after a near-perfect skate in the free program, the judges marked Orser high enough for the silver medal behind the diminutive American favourite Scott Hamilton.

Canadian downhill racers and ski-jumpers did not live up to their advance billing. On a course slowed by the heavy snowfall, Gerry Sorensen tied for sixth and Laurie Graham placed eleventh. On the men's side, Todd Brooker returned unexpectedly from his knee injury only to come in ninth, one spot behind Steve Podborski, who was well off the mark set by the surprise gold medallist, William Johnson of the United States. But these results were not nearly as disappointing as Horst Bulau's. A gold medal contender in the 70-metre event, the 21-year-old champion of 13 World Cup events finished thirty-eighth, beaten by teammate Steve Collins, who was twenty-fifth.

In the medal round of the Olympic hockey tournament, Canada lost a 4–0 battle to Czechoslovakia before going up against the undefeated Soviets. While preparing to play "the best team in the world," goaltender Mario Gosselin announced that it was his intention to keep his squad from getting "killed." For the first half of the game, he succeeded, shutting down the swirling Russian snipers with such skill that coach Dave King later pronounced Gosselin the best goalie at the Games, above even the living legend known as Tretiak. But, finally, after facing 26 shots, most of them of the point-blank variety, it was amazing that Gosselin let only four get by him. Between the pipes at the other end of the rink, it was another story. Vladislav Tretiak didn't break a sweat as he kicked away a puny total of 10 Canadian shots on goal, earning himself his first shutout in Olympic play. Canada moved from that loss to play for the bronze against Sweden. All Canada needed was a tie, but in an old, sad story the team lost 2–0 and slipped out of the medals.

In retaliation for the Moscow boycott of 1980, the Soviet Union and 13 allies, including East Germany, Cuba, and Czechoslovakia, returned the favour in the Los Angeles Summer Games of 1984. The boycotting countries cited lax security in America and the threat of anti-communist violence, and thus the Los Angeles Games lost the chance to see

Canadian swimmers accounted for 11 medals in Los Angeles. Right: Gold medallist in the 200 m breast stroke Victor Davis raises his arms in victory.

athletes from nations that had accounted for an amazing 310 medals at Montreal in 1976 — the last time a truly international, boycott-free Games had taken place.

It can't be said that the absence of hundreds of the world's best athletes hurt Canada's chances for an unprecedented number of medals including a dozen possible golds, something Canada hadn't won in summer competition since 1968. With or without the Soviets and friends, Canada had an excess of legitimate contenders: world-record-holding swimmers Alex Baumann and Victor Davis; world champion heavyweight boxer Willie de Wit and former light-middleweight champ Shawn O'Sullivan; top-ranked canoeist Larry Cain; sailor Terry McLaughlin, who would have been slotted for gold in Moscow had it not been for the boycott; the world champion synchronized swimming pair of Sharon Hambrook and Kelly Kryczka; and the heavy eight rowing crew, which under the direction of oarsman/coach Neil Campbell had upset everyone, including the Soviets and the East Germans, when they set a world record for the 2,000-metre event in Lucerne, Switzerland, a month before the Olympics were to begin.

The LA Games will always be remembered as the ultimate advertisement for "The City of Angels." The city basked in non-stop glorious sunshine and was even given a heaven-sent reprieve from its trademark smog.

Canada's first gold came courtesy of Linda Thom, an unknown 41-year-old mother of two from Ottawa who, on opening day, defeated American Ruby Fox in a tie-breaking shoot-out in the sport pistol competition. In that first week, Thom, dubbed by the media as a "pistol-packin' mama," was joined on the Canadian gold medal list by three swimmers.

It was more than appropriate that Alex Baumann had been chosen to carry the Canadian flag in the Opening Ceremonies. He went on to smash his own world record in the 400-metre medley, before claiming gold again five days later in the 200-metre version of the same event. Baumann had lost both his father and brother during the previous four years, and in a moving moment he handed his mother, who was a world-class Czech swimmer in the 1940s, a bouquet of flowers after his first victory.

Teammate Victor Davis beat his own record in the 100-metre breast stroke. Still, he finished second to American breast stroke specialist Steve Lundquist. Three nights later Davis channelled his emotional energy and emerged victorious in the 200-metre event, shaving an amazing 1.24 seconds from his previous world record. Davis added a third medal when the 4 × 100-metre relay team stroked to silver.

Breast stroker Anne Ottenbrite took home a medal in each of the three placings in 1984. She was also the first Canadian woman ever to win a swimming gold medal.

One of the nation's many unexpected medallists, 18-year-old swimmer Anne Ottenbrite from Whitby, Ontario, won three medals, one in each placing. Now a swim coach at the University of Guelph, Ottenbrite cited Baumann's performance as her inspiration for winning gold in the 200-metre breast stroke (no Canadian woman had ever won a swimming gold medal), silver in the 100-metre, bronze in the 4 × 100 medley relay, three months after dislocating her right knee while trying on a pair of shoes. Synchronized swimmer Carolyn Waldo earned a silver in the solo event, foreshadowing her double gold win in 1988.

Canada's most prominent cyclist, Steve Bauer of Fenwick, Ontario, pulled away from the pack in the 190-kilometre road race. Chased in vain by two Norwegians, Bauer and American Alexi Grewal were left alone to battle it out in the draining heat of southern California. Staying behind Bauer in order to ride in his draft and conserve

Carolyn Waldo was a 1984 silver medallist in the Olympics' first-ever synchronized swimming event; in 1988 she won two golds. Opposite: Sylvie Bernier earned Canada's first diving medal, a gold.

energy, Grewal broke away near the finish, and in the explosive sprint that ensued, the American was victorious by less than a bicycle length. Bauer's silver was more controversial than the one by teammate Curt Harnett in the one-kilometre trial because Grewal had been suspended from the U.S. Olympic team after a urine test revealed traces of the banned stimulant ephedrine. He was reinstated after an appeal.

The second week of the 1984 Summer Games was just as rewarding as the first. Diver Sylvie Bernier, a 20-year-old health sciences student, defeated the favoured American Kelly McCormick in the women's springboard competition. The pressure seemed overwhelming for Bernier's competitor, daughter of four-time Olympic champion Pat McCormick,

Curt Harnett became a three-time medal winner in Atlanta. His first Olympic race in 1984 earned him a silver medal.

and she went over too far on her usually dependable reverse two-and-a-half somersault. The sprite-like Bernier avoided the same jitters by ignoring her scores and listening to *Flashdance* on her Walkman in between dives. She maintained the lead for the last seven of her ten dives, to become the first Canadian to win an Olympic diving gold.

As legendary coach and two-time Olympian Neil Campbell stood on the shore of Lake Casitas watching his eight-man crew rip across the water, the surrounding observers could only speculate about the strategy being employed for the final race by this acknowledged technical genius. It became apparent early on, however, that Campbell's strategy was laughably simple. The crew, powered by the 26-year-old Toronto twins Mike and Mark Evans, pulled as hard and fast as they could from beginning to end. That was it. Despite a scary rush from the American and Australian crews as the Canadians grew weaker, a heart-stopping 30 seconds that saw their lead vanish over the last 250 metres, the Canadians had enough juice left to hold them off and won by a rapidly eroding 10 feet. Lake Casitas was also the site of a rowing doubles bronze for the sister act of Silken and Daniele Laumann.

Like figure skating at the Winter Olympics, boxing has consistently suffered from the subjective judging system that decides winners and losers. While the boxing disputes at the LA Games would be overshadowed by a far more contentious moment on the track, Canada was at the centre of a few heated debates in the ring. Neither Canadian heavyweight Willie de Wit, 23, of Grande Prairie, Alberta, who took silver, nor his final opponent, Henry Tillman of the United States, had been having great tournaments. Tillman had lost the bronze medal bout on points but was later given the fight after an appeal jury overruled the decision. Although de Wit had defeated Tillman twice before the Games, once by knockout, the American used a tremendously quick jab to win a 5–0 decision. But had it not been for the curious appeal, Tillman wouldn't have even had the chance to box for the gold.

Canada's most intense moment of controversy surrounded the technically gifted light middleweight Shawn O'Sullivan of Toronto. His eventual showdown with American Frank Tate was the fight boxing aficionados had been waiting for. In the final, Tate came out dancing and jabbing, trying to be anywhere except in range of O'Sullivan's devastating arsenal of punches. The first round was a close call, but in the second, O'Sullivan decked Tate hard enough for the referee to give Tate two standing eight counts, one short of a victory. Tate fought back gamely, though, jabbing effectively in the third round when O'Sullivan ignored his coach's advice and went chasing Tate around the ring. When it was announced that Tate had won the fight 5–0, O'Sullivan stood in shock in the centre of the ring, but in the post-fight interview he acted the role of the graceful loser. "There seem to be about 15,000 people out there [in the audience]

Canadian boxers were fourth overall in Los Angeles. Albertan Willie de Wit (opposite) was a silver medal winner.

Lori Fung became Canada's first medal winner in rhythmic gymnastics, with her 1984 gold in the individual event.

who disagree with the judges. I dearly wish things had gone different, but they didn't, and there's no gain in crying over spilled milk." There wasn't, but that still didn't explain how four judges gave O'Sullivan the second round by a scant 20–19 margin.

The setbacks in boxing didn't take away from the fact that to date Canada was having its best Olympics ever. It won two more gold medals that week, with Lori Fung in the new Olympic sport of rhythmic gymnastics and kayakers Hugh Fisher and Alwyn Morris in the 1,000-metre pairs. Just short of gold were sailors Terry McLaughlin and Evert Bastet, who won silver in the Flying Dutchman class, and the synchronized swimming duet of Hambrook and Kryczka, who also placed second.

Larry Cain paddled to gold in the 500 m individual canoe race at Los Angeles.

Altogether Canada won 44 medals — 10 gold, 18 silver, and 16 bronze. Two of the bronzes were especially noteworthy. Canada's little-known Ben Johnson placed third to Carl Lewis's gold in the 100-metre sprint, marking the beginning of a long rivalry that would come to a scandalous conclusion at Seoul in 1988. In the 3,000-metre race, a relatively unknown Lynn Williams won the bronze in a contest that stole headlines. The long-legged American favourite, Mary Decker, had as her chief challenger the barefoot South African, Zola Budd, who had been quickly rushed through British immigration procedures so that she could compete (South Africa had been banned from the Games since 1968). A little more than halfway through the race, the 18-year-old Budd attempted to cut in front of Decker to take the lead. Decker stepped on the back of Budd's leg and lost her balance, falling onto the infield grass where she writhed in pain after pulling a leg muscle. In the bitter aftermath, Budd came in seventh and Williams placed third.

At any other Olympic Games this would have been the quintessential Canadian moment. In a moment of folly, where the more honed foreign athletes had been disqualified by their own ambition, the unassuming Canadian quietly slipped in for third place. After the inspiration of Gaëtan Boucher, and after the Canadian gold rush at the Los Angeles Games, Canada had finally overcome its perennial also-ran complex and was now a bona fide Olympic contender.

Profile

Victor Davis

FOUR-TIME MEDALLIST, SWIMMING, 1984 AND 1988

Victor Davis never really came across as a swimmer. When he stood on the block before a race, he had the glare — not to mention the physique — of a mean pugilist limbering up before a fight. Davis came by his fighting spirit naturally. His father, Mel, had coached three boxers to the 1948 Games in London. He lived with his father following his parents' divorce and grew up in Guelph, Ontario, as a self-described "derelict." He was afraid of the water when he enrolled in swimming classes at the age of eight. It was at the Guelph Marlins Aquatic Club that Davis met his long-time coach, Clifford Barry, whom he followed when the coach moved to nearby Waterloo in 1982 and, later, Pointe-Claire, Quebec, in 1986. In all, Davis won five gold medals in international 100-metre and 200-metre breast stroke events and set two world records.

Victor Davis was an aggressive competitor who set a new world record with his gold medal 200 m win in 1984.

The record he set at the LA Games in 1984 was a testament to Davis's remarkable grit. The year leading up to the Olympics had been chaotic. Davis was charged with assault in 1983 after a fight had broken out at his home in Waterloo during a late-night party. While waiting for the trial, he battled a severe case of mononucleosis. The assault charges were later dismissed, but the following spring, with the Olympics only a few months away, he became afflicted with a bad sciatic nerve condition. The fact that, in June, at the Canadian Olympic trials in Etobicoke, Davis broke his own 200-metre breast stroke record was mind-boggling.

Davis and his coach kept it a secret that 10 days before the Olympic meet, Davis had sprained his right ankle climbing over a bicycle stand. Barry was mortified by the accident and feared that Davis would be swimming well below his standard, adding seconds to his time. Davis, on the other hand, was less than concerned. His coach was even unable to talk him out of playing hacky-sack on the California beach with a bandaged foot just three days later.

Expert commentators, who had no idea about Davis's recent injury, were dumbfounded when he took more than a full second off the 200-metre world record at the LA Games to win the gold in 2:13.34. It was a record that stood for nearly five years.

Three months after American Michael Barrowman lowered the record to 2:12.90 in August 1989, Victor Davis died tragically after being struck by a car outside a Montreal bar. Just after midnight on November 11, Davis and his 22-year-old girlfriend, Donna Clavel, and another friend, Jennifer Watt, left the establishment in the quiet suburb of Ste-Anne-de-Bellevue. When Davis went across the street to buy some orange juice, three men who had been in the bar began shouting at the two young women as they waited in Davis's car. Davis didn't hesitate to chase them away, but they soon returned, this time inside a black 1989 Honda. Although exactly what happened next is unclear, it is fair to say that Davis was standing in the car's path and, as it approached, he hurled a large glass container at the windshield. The car struck him, throwing his limp body more than 30 feet. He landed head first on top of a parked car and died within hours.

The driver of the Honda, then 19-year-old Glen Crossley, was sentenced to 10 months in jail for leaving the scene of an accident in February 1992. Crossley appealed the conviction and did not serve the sentence. As of February 1995, the Quebec Court of Appeal had not yet rendered its ruling.

Davis had been named a member of the Order of Canada in 1985. He failed to qualify for the 200-metre breast stroke event at the 1988 Seoul Olympics, but was the driving force behind the 4 x 100-metre relay team's silver medal. It seemed fitting that in his final Olympic race, Davis clocked the fastest split for the breast stroke ever recorded, 1:00.9. He retired from competitive swimming on July 5, 1989, and started a Montreal-based swimming pool safety company and a lifeguard placement service.

In the days following Davis's death, about 200 friends and associates gathered at coach Clifford Barry's home in Quebec to toast the popular athlete. "Victor was the greatest guy," said his former coach. "He had the most incredible effect on those people he touched." This was undeniably true, but it seemed only too appropriate that Davis had gone out with a fight.

CHAPTER EIGHT

SHAME
in SEOUL,
CELEBRATION
in CALGARY

THE GAMES OF 1988

KAREN O'REILLY

NINETEEN EIGHTY-EIGHT WAS THE YEAR CANADA OCCUPIED CENTRE STAGE at both the Summer Games in Seoul, Korea, and the Winter Games in Calgary, Alberta. It was the year Canadians showed the rest of the world that when we are good, we are very, very good. And when we are bad, we are horrid.

After the fact, you'd have to wonder why the IOC ever decided to select Calgary as the site for the 1988 Winter Olympics. The city had no facilities to speak of. Its hockey rink was 30 years old. It had been over 12 years since a major new ski area had been developed anywhere in the province of Alberta. And nowhere in the province were there facilities for track speed-skating, bobsledding, or luging. There is some question whether the international media knew whom they were championing, even *after* Calgary won the bid in 1981. The mayor of Cagliari, capital city of Sardinia, Italy, received several telegrams of congratulations in the weeks following the IOC's announcement.

Money was a problem, too. The Calgary Olympic Organizing Committee, which decided against the acronym of COOC in favour of OCO '88, started operations with $35,000 in seed money from the Calgary Booster Club. The Committee estimated it would cost $212 million to stage the Calgary Games, plus the cost of building new facilities.

To raise the money they needed, OCO '88 members launched tireless fund-raisers over the decade preceding the Games. They held a $1,000-a-plate dinner, and over 600 people attended. They flipped thousands of pancakes. And they developed funding partnerships with the City of Calgary, the Province of Alberta, and the Government of Canada.

And so, on February 13, 1988, over 60,000 spectators gathered in the newly renovated McMahon Stadium to see the Olympic torch carried its last few feet by Robyn Perry, a local seventh-grader and figure skater. The fifteenth Olympic Winter Games were officially opened, hosting a record number of 1,750 athletes from a record 57 nations.

And what had all the pancake breakfasts, give-away cowboy hats, Calgary spirit, Alberta grit, and Canadian pride produced? State-of-the-art facilities like no other Winter Games had ever enjoyed: the Canmore Nordic Centre, Canada Olympic Park, Nakiska Alpine Ski Area, Olympic Speed Skating Oval, the Olympic Saddledome, Father David Bauer Arena, Calgary Olympic Village, Canmore Olympic Village, Olympic Plaza, and a media village. Upgraded facilities included the Max Bell Arena, McMahon Stadium, Norma Bush Arena, and Jimmie Condon Arena.

One thing even Calgary's crackerjack organizers couldn't organize was the weather. During Opening Ceremonies a chinook blew in, putting the lie to OCO's written guarantee to the International Olympic Committee that Calgary would provide "incomparable real winter weather. It is reliable weather, plentiful snow, no rain, no fog, and a long, long season — ideal conditions for training of our best athletes."

Brian Orser proudly ushers in the Canadian team at the 1988 Calgary Games (opposite). Spectators sunbathe at the Alpine event finish line, basking in the warmth of a chinook that caused the rescheduling of many events.

From the first day of events to the end of the Closing Ceremonies, the strongest winds in 25 years were recorded for Calgary. Gale force chinook winds reached 160 kilometres an hour the first day of outdoor competition. The snow was licked clean away in some spots, and spectators took off their shirts to get a suntan. The temperature swung wildly from 28 degrees below zero Celsius, to 22 degrees above.

A total of 33 events had to be rescheduled, which involved ticket redistribution, changing bus transportation, moving camera crews around, and reordering food services. Alpine skiing and ski-jumping were the sports most affected.

Despite the horrible conditions, Canada's first medal of the Games went to Karen Percy for her third-place finish in the women's downhill. It had been a difficult day for the feisty skier from Edmonton. Two weeks earlier, Percy had taken first place in both the giant slalom and the super giant slalom (Super G) at the national championships. Expectations were high, and Canadians were itchy for a win by the sixth day of competition. Percy held the lead until the last 10 nail-biting minutes of competition when the gold went to Marina Kiehl of West Germany and the silver to Brigitte Oertli of Switzerland.

Percy won the bronze again three days later for her performance in the women's Super G event, behind Sigrid Wolf from Austria (gold) and Michela Figini of Switzerland (silver). Canada hadn't had an alpine skier win double medals for 20 years, since Nancy Greene won gold and silver at the 1968 Winter Games in Grenoble, France.

Every Olympic Games carries with it the promise of glory and the risk of disappointment. Perhaps no disappointment was greater for Canada than its poor showing in the 12-nation hockey tournament. The team from the Soviet Union dominated the rink through all preliminary-round play. On February 24, the Soviets shut out Canada 5–0 and eliminated any hopes we might have had for a medal. The U.S.S.R. won the gold, with seven wins and one loss.

Another letdown came with speed-skater Gaëtan Boucher's performance. Boucher was our most decorated sports champion going into the 1988 Winter Olympics. He'd won the silver medal in the 1,000 metres at Lake Placid in 1980 and, four years later, two golds in the 1,000 and 1,500 metres and a bronze in the 500 metres at Sarajevo. Lacing up his skates, Boucher said that Calgary would be his final Winter Olympics. "I want to retire in a blaze of glory." It was not to be. Speed-skaters from Sweden, East Germany, and the U.S.S.R. took the three top spots.

Downhiller Karen Percy was the first Canadian medal winner of the Calgary Games with a time of 1:26.62, 1/100ths of a second behind silver medallist Brigitte Oertli.

However, skating of a different sort gave Canada some of its finest moments, not to mention the honour of three more medals. In what came to be known as "The Battle of the Brians," Brian Orser from Penetanguishene, Ontario, and Brian Boitano from the United States took to the ice before a packed house at the Olympic Saddledome to fight for the gold in men's figure skating. Orser, already a silver medallist in Sarajevo, once said, "Skates are my voice, the ice is my instrument." The voice was off on this day, and Orser stumbled once or twice in an otherwise brilliant performance. He collected the second and final silver of his amateur career. Boitano captured the gold.

Canada's next skating medal, in ice dancing, went to Tracy Wilson of Port Moody, British Columbia, and Rob McCall of Dartmouth, Nova Scotia. Ice dancing was first introduced to the Winter Games in 1976, and since then the Soviets had won six of nine possible medals. Wilson and McCall, clearly the darlings of the crowd, especially when they danced to "The Maple Leaf Rag," provided enough of a shakeup to win a bronze medal, sharing the podium with two Soviet couples.

The surprise win of the Games, at least from a Canadian point of view, came from Elizabeth Manley in the women's figure skating. Manley went into the competition suffering from many ailments, but, more significantly, the contest was viewed as strictly a two-woman affair: Katarina Witt of Germany versus American Debi Thomas. Manley had held on for third place overall in compulsory figures and the short program. On the climactic night of the long program, Manley skated the performance of her life. The judges awarded her the gold medal for free skating, and overall, Manley came within a fraction of a point of taking the gold medal from Witt. Manley settled for the silver with Thomas getting the bronze.

The 1988 Winter Olympics yielded a total of five medals for Canada. There was considerable soul-searching over the fact that none of the 117 Canadian athletes who took part won a gold in any of the 46 events. However, 19 Canadians placed high with top-eight finishes, a better overall rating than ever before. And, in the four demonstration sports — curling, freestyle skiing, short-track speed-skating, and disabled skiing — Canadians finished first, second, and

Brian Orser came a proud second in the "Battle of the Brians" against U.S. skater Brian Boitano. Left: Tracy Wilson and Rob McCall were the first Canadians to win a medal in ice dancing, an event in which the Soviets dominated with eight out of twelve medals between 1976 and 1988.

third place more than a dozen times, with an especially strong showing in speed-skating. The top three winners of the 1988 Winter Games were the Soviet Union with 29 medals, including 11 gold; East Germany with 25 medals, 9 gold; and Switzerland with 15 medals, 5 gold.

The Seoul Olympics were the first Summer Games since 1972 not marred by a major boycott. The United States, the Soviet Bloc countries, and China were free to go at one another head-to-head. Fresh off the highly praised Calgary Winter Olympics, Canadians were determined to make their mark, too.

In September 1988 we began shipping a huge team of 386 Canadian athletes, 140 coaches and trainers, tons of equipment, horses, running shoes, ear plugs, and at least one 2,200-pound boat to Seoul. Ours was the fourth-largest team at the Games, which hosted 9,600 athletes from 160 countries.

The Canadian media went into overdrive, combing records for potential winners, betting careers on predicted outcomes, sending home lively accounts of life in Seoul. Most touched on the ever-present "threat" from North Korea, only 48 kilometres away from Seoul, beyond a demilitarized zone established in 1953 at the end of the Korean War. For the Games, no one was taking any chances. There were 63 armed personnel for every athlete and official guest, including 120,000 anti-terrorist fighters, 700,000 Korean armed forces personnel, 40,000 U.S. soldiers and marines, 10,000 U.S. sailors aboard aircraft carriers patrolling the coast, plus American spy satellites monitoring North Korean troop movements.

Despite the ever-present racket of patrolling ships, planes, and helicopters, the citizens of Seoul were anxious not to offend Western sensibilities. People caught spitting in the street, a common Korean practice, were thrown in jail for 29 days until the Games were safely over. Authorities tried to ban the sale of dog and snake meat, without much success. Korean men favour dog meat, eels, and raw eggs for their supposed contribution to sexual stamina. Not that stamina was much in demand: city police banned Seoul's *kissaeng* girls ("relaxation guaranteed") from their barbershop perches for the duration of the Games.

Canadian sportswriters laid their bets that we had a strong chance of success in swimming, the sport that had given us 10 medals in Los Angeles. Veteran Victor Davis was touted, along with Allison Higson, already the 200-metre

Elizabeth Manley was the first Canadian woman to win a figure skating medal since 1972, when Karen Magnussen, like Manley, captured silver.

Going into the Seoul Olympics, sprinter Ben Johnson was already a world record holder in the 100 m.

women's breast stroke world-record holder. Instead, synchronized swimming turned out to be a Canadian triumph. Our success in boxing was an accurate prediction, with Cuba, the top-ranked country, being one of the few no-shows in Seoul. But mostly, we were 100 percent sure of our Bens.

Big Ben, a 12-year-old, 17.3-hand chestnut gelding from Belgium, was sent to enter the equestrian show jumping events, backed by a gold medal victory at the Pan-American Games in 1987. His rider, Ian Millar, was a handsome part-time farmer and stockbroker from Perth, Ontario. Going into the Games, Millar was the number one ranked show jumper in the world.

But it was not Big Ben's Olympics. Individual and team jumping medals went to the United States, France, and West Germany. Instead, Canada won a bronze medal in team dressage thanks to Emirage, Malte, Reipo, and Dynasty. Their riders, in the same order: Eva-Maria Pracht of Cedar Valley, Ontario; Gina Smith of Saskatoon, Saskatchewan; Ashley Nicoll of Toronto, Ontario; and Cindy Ishoy of Hamilton, Ontario.

That left the other Ben. Ben Johnson had already made his mark with a bronze medal in the men's 100-metre relay at Los Angeles. Three short years later, he flew to a new world record of 9.83 seconds in the men's 100-metre event in August 1987, at

Ben Johnson pulls ahead of the pack for his ultimately disqualified win, which threw the Canadian amateur sports world into an intense period of self-scrutiny.

the World Outdoor Championships in Rome. Johnson was now Canada's greatest hope for an Olympic gold in the Games' single most prestigious event.

On September 24, in Seoul, Johnson beat arch-rival Carl Lewis in the men's 100-metre event with a time of 9.79. Canadians coast to coast went wild in a boundless orgy of self-congratulation, and Johnson became an instant hero and role model for kids everywhere. The letdown and sense of betrayal were equally extreme when, on September 27, the IOF announced that two urine samples taken from Johnson contained stanozolol, an anabolic steroid. At three o'clock in the morning a Canadian Olympic official knocked on Johnson's hotel room door and collected his gold medal, which went to Carl Lewis.

Part of the reason for Canadians' supreme ecstasy when Johnson won the gold on September 24 was that we hadn't managed to win a single medal in the first week of the Games. The sole exception turned out to be our only medal in the three demonstration sports of baseball, women's judo, and tae kwon do. Yvonne Frassen, from Wallaceburg, Ontario, won the bronze for her skill in tae-kwon do, a martial art developed in Korea.

Canadians were especially upset by a lack of performance in the swimming pool. The star of the show was clearly turning out to be U.S. swimmer Matt Biondi, who went on to win five gold medals, a silver, and a bronze. Ominously, our other possible source of medals — weightlifting competition — had taken place without four of Canada's seven-man team. They had been disqualified after testing positive for anabolic steroids.

So, when Johnson stepped up to the podium, we felt a curse had been lifted. At last, a medal! Later the same day, we knew we were safely out of the doldrums when

Sailor Larry Lemieux was a true hero of the Seoul Games, when he left his second-place position to rescue injured Singaporean boaters. Below: Frank McLaughlin and John Millen give thumbs up for their bronze yachting win.

the Canadian women's swim team won a bronze in the 100-metre medley relay. Allison Higson from Brampton, Jane Kerr from Mississauga, and Lori Melien from London, all in Ontario, along with Andrea Nugent from Calgary — achieved a Canadian Senior Record with a finish time of 4:10.49.

At Pusan, 300 kilometres south of Seoul, another Canadian was battling dangerous and unpredictable seas in the seven-race Finn yachting competition. Lawrence

Lemieux, from Edmonton, was running second in his race when he spotted a capsized boat from a previous race. The Singapore crew members were in trouble, and one had injured his back. Lemieux fell out of his race to rescue the sailors. It was an heroic effort and Lemieux was awarded a second-place finish, despite sailing into port in twenty-first place. At the time, Canadians were too dizzy with Johnson's win to fully appreciate Lemieux's selfless act of bravery.

Backstroker Mark Tewksbury was a member of the silver-winning medley relay team in 1988. In 1992 he struck gold in the 100 m race.

Our bliss continued the following day when the Canadian dressage team won a bronze medal, and the men's swim team took silver in the 4 × 100-metre medley relay. Victor Davis from Guelph and Sandy Goss from Toronto, along with Tom Ponting and Mark Tewksbury, both from Calgary, placed in a tight, three-way competition seconds ahead of the Soviet Union and seconds behind the winning U.S. team. On September 27, Canadian sailors Frank McLaughlin and John Millen, both from Toronto, braved three-metre waves to win a bronze medal behind Denmark (gold) and Norway (silver) in the Flying Dutchman yachting competition. The water was very deep, and there were strong currents and nasty winds.

In the week following Johnson's disgrace, Canada won another six Olympic medals, including three more golds to replace the one we lost. Sadly, praise was muted for these achievements. Canadian athletes at the Seoul Olympic Village were regular targets of finger-pointing and many were ostracized, which added to the pressure of performance. Sprinter Mark McKoy packed up and left for home. With both Johnson and McKoy out of the men's 100-metre relay competition, our hopes for a medal were dashed.

Two days later, on September 29, Canadians were treated to a rare accomplishment in men's track and field. Decathlete Dave Steen, 28 years old, from Burnaby, British

Columbia, racked up 8,328 points over the two-day decathlon event to win a bronze.

Each day, Steen got up at 4 A.M. for warm-up exercises in the Olympic Village courtyard, to be ready for the 8:30 A.M. start time. The first day's events included a 100-metre race, the long jump, shotput, and high jump, followed by the 400-metre dash. Steen was known as a well-coordinated, all-round athlete, but he also had long legs and a terrific natural jumping ability, which served him well in the long jump and high jump.

Something else Steen was exceptionally good at was keeping his cool. His former coach, Andy Higgins at the University of Toronto, once described him as a completely "self-actualized" human being. "He doesn't have to prove anything," said Higgins. In fact, Steen was so cool his trainers once decided to test his ability to withstand tension by attaching electrodes to his body during a particularly gruelling competition. They discovered that, at the height of the test, Steen was in a deeply relaxed state. "The challenge was always to get Dave excited enough to compete," said Higgins.

Dave Steen went down in Canadian Olympic history when he won our first-ever medal, a bronze, in the decathlon. The two-day competition combines 10 running, jumping and throwing events.

The second day's events began with a 110-metre hurdles race, followed by discus throwing, the pole vault, and javelin hurling. Steen did well, though tension was rising with his eighth-place finish going into the final event — the long, hot, 1,500-metre race. Tension for spectators, that is. Steen breezed through the race, cool as a cucumber, to fix himself solidly in third place. He finished 160 points behind the first-place winner Christian Schenk, from East Germany. The silver medal went to Torsten Voss, also from East Germany.

Before gliding into the water, Carolyn Waldo, a synchronized swimmer from Beaconsfield, Quebec, had said of the Johnson scandal: "It has given us more of a spark to go in there and win gold medals for Canada." With just days to go before the end of the Games, Waldo swept the field with a gold medal in the solo event on September 30 and a gold medal in the duet, with partner Michelle Cameron from Calgary, on

149

October 1. Waldo became the first woman in Canadian history to win two gold medals at a single Summer Games.

Also on October 1, another remarkable performance by Egerton Marcus of Toronto gave Canada a silver in the middleweight (165 pounds) boxing final. Going

into competition, Marcus had been touted as a strong contender, especially for his powerful right. He had broken his right hand in a quarter-final bout and his opponent in the final, Henry Maske from East Germany, knew of his injury. Marcus decided to surprise Maske by swinging hard with his right for most of the first round, and Maske was taken aback. But Marcus paid for his strategy. He hadn't taken any pain killers for fear of another doping scandal. By the second round, he could no longer feel his right hand at all. Lesser boxers would have quit, but Marcus battled on for silver.

On the final day of the Games, Canada gathered up a bronze medal from Ray Downey of Halifax, Nova Scotia, in the 156-pound light middleweight boxing final, and a gold medal from Lennox Lewis in the 201-plus pounds heavyweight final. Lewis, from Kitchener, Ontario, was the first Canadian boxer to win a gold since 1932.

The top three winners of the 1988 Summer Olympics in Seoul were the Soviet Union with 132, including 55 gold, medals; East Germany with 102 medals, 37 gold; and the United States with 94 medals, 36 gold. Canada came out of Seoul with 10 medals in six sports, and overall, we reached the finals in 15 of 23 sports. Not a bad showing, but one that was totally overshadowed by the Ben Johnson scandal, a shameful episode in Canadian sports history that would haunt the country for years to come.

Canadians captured medals in all three placings in boxing at Seoul and tied for fourth overall. Light middle-weight Ray Downey was a bronze medallist who later became three-time national champion. Heavyweight fighter Lennox Lewis (right) earned the first Canadian gold in boxing since 1932.

Synchro swimmer Carolyn Waldo had reason to rejoice in her history-making double-gold win.

Profile

Elizabeth Manley

SILVER MEDALLIST, FIGURE SKATING, 1988

Right after the Opening Ceremonies in Calgary in 1988, Elizabeth Manley flew back to Ottawa, her home town, to train for her run at the figure skating gold medal in calm and isolation. Her departure from the Olympic site turned a few heads, but few knew that Manley was suffering from fever, flu, and infected ears. In her practice sessions, she had felt unstable and feared the antibiotics she was taking for her various ailments were causing the imbalance she was experiencing on the ice.

Her condition deteriorated on the plane trip from Ottawa back to Calgary, a journey that Manley describes as "among my all-time worst experiences." The only route available was a traveller's nightmare — Ottawa to Toronto, Toronto to Thunder Bay, Thunder Bay to Saskatoon, Saskatoon to Calgary. For Manley, the changes in air pressure from so many takeoffs and landings were excruciating, and flight attendants poured warm oil into her throbbing ears, trying to ease the pain.

Olympic doctors in Calgary diagnosed strep throat, accompanied by high fever, in addition to her severe ear infection. Apart from a cough suppressant, there was little doctors could prescribe within Olympic drug regulations. Manley took all of this in brave stride — until she stepped on the ice for a practice session a couple of days before the start of competition. She realized immediately that her balance was way off, that she couldn't properly trace a figure on the ice. This was the last straw, and Manley burst into tears.

Though she was only 22 years old at the time, Manley had already faced some difficult challenges in her life. She describes herself as an "army brat," the first daughter and youngest child of Joan and Bernard Manley. When the family was transferred to Ottawa, Manley was nine and so serious about her skating career that she trained 18 hours a week. Her mother believed in Manley's potential from the start and spent hours sewing costumes, driving her to practice sessions, and earning extra money to pay expenses.

By the time Manley was 12, her parents had drifted apart. Though she enjoys good relations with both parents today, Manley suffered a severe bout of depression in her late teens. In her typically upbeat way, Manley has made the best of her depressive episode and has acted as national spokesperson for the Canadian Mental Health Association.

Money was a constant worry for Manley and her mother. Her coaches helped. One used to sneak Manley into an arena to practise in the off-hours, and another paid her $10 every time she

Elizabeth Manley gave the performance of her career at the Calgary Saddledome when she won Canadians' hearts with her silver medal skate.

mastered a new, intricate school figure. The Canadian Figure Skating Association and Sport Canada eventually chipped in with meaningful financial support. Still, when Manley wobbled on to the ice in Calgary, her mother's debt stood at what seemed an insurmountable $26,000.

For the first time in her career, Manley felt defeated, saying she couldn't compete. Her co-trainer Peter Dunfield persuaded Manley to get out on the ice one more time, to take one more practice skate. After watching the skater closely, he called her over and examined her blades, to find one of the settings out of whack. Once Manley knew it was her skate that was causing the balance trouble, not her health, she felt a return of her usual optimism and set her sights back on a medal win.

Meanwhile, the Olympic audience was enthralled by the contest developing between Katarina Witt and Debi Thomas. Both women had chosen music from Bizet's *Carmen* for their long routines, causing them to be dubbed the "Duelling Carmens." But only one could take gold, which went to Witt, while Manley skated brilliantly and won the silver, leaving the bronze to Thomas.

Both of Manley's parents were in the audience at the Saddledome, which went wild after her performance. "It was wonderful to be able to share the victory with Mom who had worked so hard for this moment and never once lost hope. And it was also a great feeling that I had finally proved to Dad what it had been all about. I felt, at last, that he was really proud of me."

Some months later, after signing with the Ice Capades, Elizabeth Manley marched down to the bank and paid off all $26,000 of her mother's debt.

CHAPTER NINE

HEROES and HEARTBREAK

THE GAMES OF 1992

STEVEN MILTON

FOR SEVEN DECADES, THERE WAS A COSY, QUADRENNIAL RHYTHM TO THE Olympic movement. Whenever there was a Winter Games, a Summer Games would be close on its heels: three and a half years gradually mounting to two Olympics in eight frenetic months; a mammoth letdown; another slow buildup. But 1992 was a watershed Olympics, the last time that the Winter and Summer events were held in the same year. Because they were cheaper to stage, the Winter Olympics were scheduled to resurface first at Lillehammer, Norway, in 1994, launching a separate four-year cycle for the ice and snow events, and leaving the older and more prestigious Summer Olympics to their normal rotation. Advertising and administrative resources would be planned more evenly, poorer countries could spread out travel costs, and total revenues would presumably skyrocket.

Kerrin Lee-Gartner (centre) became the first Canadian woman to win Olympic downhill gold, which she took by a 6/100ths of a second margin in Albertville.

In this final year of cohabitation, it was almost as if the International Olympic Committee wanted the two Olympics close enough to kiss each other goodbye. Not since the Oslo and Helsinki Games, 40 years earlier, had a Winter and Summer Games been held in such tight geographical proximity as Albertville, France, and Barcelona, Spain. In fact, after that Scandinavian double-header, the two Games had not even shared the same continent.

For Canadians, the Albertville Winter Games and Barcelona Summer Games were linked by more than just the calendar and a map of Europe. There were also thematic similarities. For instance, debilitating injuries fettered Canadian champions in both winter and summer: figure skater Kurt Browning at Albertville and rower Silken Laumann in Barcelona. At both Games, the Canadian women's teams turned in decisive, stimulating victories, the short-track speed-skaters in the winter and the rowers in the summer. And in yet another continuing theme, Canadian athletes came from out of nowhere in both Albertville and Barcelona to produce stunning medal performances: a bronze in the 86-kilogram judo event by Montreal's Nicolas Gill; a silver by race-walker Guillaume Leblanc of Sept-Isles, Quebec; another silver for Jeff Thue, Canada's first freestyle wrestling medal in a non-boycott year since 1936; and a gold in the downhill by Kerrin Lee-Gartner of Rossland, British Columbia.

The redemption theme was also common to Canadian contingents at both Games. A tough new reality was affecting the Games. The sunny "Going for Gold" campaign that peaked in 1988 and did not yield a single Olympic championship in Calgary was being shouldered aside by a hard-line results-or-else approach. Athletes at the Summer Olympics were also determined to rid themselves of the stigma of the Seoul steroid scandal. Chef de mission Ken Read, the former Crazy Canucks skiing ace, said there was something to prove: "That Canadians can play well, play fair, and play clean."

And there were successes, many of them, although at times the disappointments seemed to overshadow the accomplishments. The celebrated figure skaters could do no better than one bronze medal. Five-time world champion Sylvie Daigle was fouled and did not make it out of her short-track speed-skating heat. The injury-plagued men's downhillers crashed and burned. Gymnast Curtis Hibbert, a two-time medallist at the world championships, didn't qualify for any finals. And on a single day in Barcelona, decathlon hopeful Michael Smith withdrew with a hamstring injury, world champion kayaker Renn Crichlow failed to qualify for the 500-metre final, and Sylvie Fréchette saw her gold medal chances in synchronized swimming evaporate when a judge punched the wrong computer button.

But Canadians could also argue that this was among their best Olympics ever. The Winter team took home two golds, three silvers, and two bronzes, the seven medals equalling the 1932 Games as our best Winter total. And the Summer team's 18-medal haul included six gold (upped to seven when Fréchette was awarded a retroactive gold the following year), ranking behind only the boycott-reduced '84 Los Angeles Games and the 22 medals won in Atlanta.

There were no major boycotts at either '92 Olympics. In fact, there were record registrations at both. The disintegration of the Soviet Bloc had created some new countries and resurrected old ones. Beginning with Albertville, Germany had a unified team for the first time since 1964, although internal bickering and smouldering mistrust between east and west factions were rampant. Former Soviet republics

A scoring error cost synchro swimmer Sylvie Fréchette gold in Barcelona. One judge misrecorded Fréchette's score, and the mistake was not rectified until 16 months after the Games, when the Canadian was retroactively awarded a gold medal.

Four-time world champion figure skater Kurt Browning ruefully accepted his disappointing sixth-place finish at Albertville.

Latvia, Lithuania, Estonia, and the Ukraine flew their own flags. Czechoslovakia was permitted one flag, but a compound name: the Czech and Slovak Federative Republic. Five Soviet republics (12 in the Summer Games) were lumped under a temporary umbrella as the Unified Team, an impersonal, generic term that pleased no one, but that resulted in a last-gasp string of Olympic successes for the crumbled Russian Empire. The Albertville Games attracted entries from 64 countries, while Barcelona welcomed 172 nations. Barcelona was the first Summer Games in 20 years from which no nation abstained. The North Koreans and Cubans were on board for the first time since 1980, and after an absence of 32 years, South Africa was back, thanks to the repeal of its anti-apartheid laws.

While the last of the same-year Olympics became the first of the new order, there was a huge difference in the ambiance, both environmental and Olympian, between the two hosting cities. Barcelona, at 17,000 people per square kilometre, is Europe's most crowded city, a double boiler of summer heat and smog. But it is also cosmopolitan and had undergone $8 billion of improvements; its night spots stayed open until dawn, and there was a strong sense of Olympic fever. Especially if you counted an 1,800-person jet-set Olympic party hosted by King Juan Carlos and Queen Sofia that included Princess Anne, Fidel Castro, and Arnold Schwarzenegger.

Albertville, on the other hand, while not pretty itself (it is the region's industrial and commercial traffic centre), was surrounded by the majesty of the French Alps. Some of the skiing venues, particularly Val d'Isère, were postcard settings, but overall the Games lacked feeling and charm. Some structures, like the skating rink and the stadium for the Opening and Closing Ceremonies, were little more than giant Meccano sets, temporary edifices scheduled for dismantling when the Games ended. Events were dispersed over 13 scattered venues, separated by hundreds of kilometres of mountain roads and switchbacks, erecting barriers between various arms of the Olympic community. There were fears that this was a harbinger of the future, an Olympics spread over such vast distances that they could be fully taken in only on television.

The Albertville Olympics were the Games of the Italian skier Alberto Tomba (two golds), figure skating gold medallist Kristi Yamaguchi (an American who trained in Edmonton), Finnish triple-medallist ski-jumper Toni Nieminen, and triple-gold cross-country skier Lyubov Egorova from the Unified Team. And of homespun American speed-skater Bonnie Blair, who followed up her Calgary gold medal with two more gold medals.

But Albertville was also the Olympics of a gritty Canadian skier named Kerrin Lee-Gartner. By the time Lee-Gartner stood in the starter's gate the middle Saturday of the Games, flagging Canadian spirits were desperate for a jump-start. Biathlete Myriam Bédard had been only twelfth in the 7.5-kilometre competition, her best event. The bobsledders were in turmoil because the selection of the two-man team was left until the last minute. The figure skaters, of whom so much had been expected, were reduced to just one medal, a bronze from Isabelle Brasseur and Lloyd Eisler, who had hoped to challenge for gold. Four-time world champion Kurt Browning — skating well below optimum conditioning because of a back injury that had kept him off blades for four months— fell on his triple Axel in the short program and was fourth, on his way to a disastrous sixth place. "As a Canadian and a sports fan, I'm disappointed," rued Browning,

Short-track speed-skater Fréderic Blackburn was a surprise silver medallist at the 1992 Winter Games.

who saw his long-time rival Viktor Petrenko of Ukraine skate a stale program but still get the gold ahead of unheralded American Paul Wylie, who many observers thought should have won.

Canadian Elvis Stojko had skated the most technically proficient short program of any of the men but was marked sixth. Stojko wowed the audience with yet another superb jump-fest two nights later, but elicited only wait-your-turn yawns from the judges, who inexcusably dropped him one place to seventh. And ice dancer Jacqueline Petr suffered a 22-stitch cut in a bizarre fall in practice, limiting the moves she and partner Mark Janoschak could perform. Because pain-killers were on the anti-doping list, Petr had to fight intense pain with only a local anaesthetic.

On the ski hills, the men's downhillers were in rough shape. They got only an eighteenth from Felix Belczyk; Rob Boyd was out with a knee injury; Edi Podivinsky fell and tore ligaments during practice; and Brian Stemmle finished twenty-third. In luge, ski-jumping, and cross-country skiing, Canada was producing poor results for a variety of reasons — injuries, a shortage of international experience, lack of strong coaching and dedicated practice and, in some cases, possibly plain shortage of talent.

Kerrin Lee-Gartner was unfazed by the daunting challenges of the Roc de Fer downhill course at Albertville, site of her unexpected first-place finish.

Canadian chef de mission Walter Sieber intimated that some of these sports might not be represented at Lillehammer, thereby creating a huge backlash of resentment among team members.

These winds of depression still swirled around the Canadian contingent when Lee-Gartner tripped the timing gate at the top of Roc de Fer, one of the toughest women's Olympic downhill courses ever. One jump was nicknamed "noodles" because it twisted skiers into spaghetti-like knots. No Canadian woman had ever won Olympic downhill gold, and few handicappers granted Lee-Gartner much of a chance. Her previous best international finish had been a World Cup third earlier in the year, and these same Alps were the site of a horrific crash she had suffered at Val d'Isère in 1986, which necessitated knee surgery and eight months of physiotherapy.

But Lee-Gartner has a skiing pedigree. She grew up in Rossland, British Columbia, just a few doors from Nancy Greene, the icon of Canadian skiing, and was influenced heavily by the Greene mystique. She skied Red Mountain, Greene's hill. She married a skiing expert, Austrian-born Max Gartner, who had coached the Canadian women's team. And she was skiing a treacherous course, the kind that a previous wave of Canadian downhillers— the Crazy Canucks of the early '80s — relished.

"About a year and a half ago, I woke up and I'd had a dream that somebody was saying 'Medaille d'Or, Kerrin Lee-Gartner... Canada,' and I don't even speak

French," Lee-Gartner recalled. Her skis did her talking for her as she whipped down the Roc de Fer in 1:52.55 seconds, .06 seconds better than another long shot, American Hilary Lindh, and .09 ahead of Austrian Veronika Wallinger to give Canada its first Winter Games' gold since Gaëtan Boucher at Sarajevo in 1984.

Things were definitely looking up for Canada, although one more setback remained. Five-time world champion Sylvie Daigle — hoping to become the gold medallist in short-track speed-skating's Olympic debut— was eliminated in her heat after bullish American Cathy Turner, the eventual gold medallist, cut inside her and clipped Daigle's skate, bending the blade.

Daigle, who had personified short-track in Canada, finally got her gold when she skated the final leg for the women's relay team. When she looked behind her to ensure that she was home free on the final lap, it was Turner she saw in the distance. "It was probably the last chance for me," said Daigle, who planned to enter medical school. "It is the perfect end to our dream." Not to be outdone, the men's team won two silvers, one by little-known Fréderic Blackburn in the singles, the other by the relay team.

Myriam Bédard, meanwhile, was about to make biathlon a recognizable word in Canada. She rallied from her frustration in the 7.5-kilometre race to nail a bronze in the 15 kilometres. Just 22, Bédard dif-fered from other world-class biathlon-ers by taking up shooting first, as an army cadet, before learning how to ski. The cart-before-the-horse approach helped Bédard more easily master the biathlon's most difficult transition: stilling the adrenalin rush of skiing enough to focus on a tiny target 50 metres away. "You have to calm your heart in a hurry," Bédard said.

The Canadian women's short-track speed-skating relay team bask in the glory of a gold-medal finish.

Hockey fans had to calm their hearts during the Canadian hockey team's quarter-final tussle with Germany. Expected to be a walkover —Canada had finished first in its group, the Germans fourth in theirs — the game went to over-time, then a sudden-death shoot-out. Canada won 4–3, thanks to Eric Lindros scor-ing the winner and some brilliant goaltending by Sean Burke, who got a pad on Peter

Draisaitl's shot to send Canada into the semi-final.

The Canadian team had a few bona fide NHL prospects in Lindros and centre Joe Juneau, who won the tournament scoring title, plus a few veterans like Dave Hannan and Burke who'd played in the big leagues but otherwise were described as "ditch-diggers and plumbers."

After a 4–2 semi-final win over the Czechs, Canada faced the Unified Team in the battle for the gold medal, which had eluded Canadian Olympians since 1952. Before the final, the team received 30,000 messages of support at its residence in the village of

Silken Laumann was unquestionably the Canadian heroine of the Barcelona Games, when she rowed to a bronze medal in spite of recent and devastating injuries to her leg.

La Tania. The game was tied at zero through two periods but the Unified Team, in one of its most satisfying performances ever, outscored the Canadians 3–1, coming home to win yet another gold. The silver was Canada's first hockey medal since a bronze in 1968 and best finish since a silver behind the U.S.'s first "Miracle on Ice" in 1960.

As Albertville drew to a close on a positive note, and Canadians began to look ahead to Barcelona, our top two medal hopes were clearly synchronized swimmer Sylvie Fréchette and rower Silken Laumann, defending world champions in their respective sports. But when the Summer Olympic flame was doused, Fréchette was carrying a silver medal and Laumann wore bronze. However, the courage behind those two medals was far richer than their hue.

Ten weeks before the Olympics, Laumann was severely injured during a training session when a German boat rammed hers. Doctors predicted she would be unable to compete in Barcelona and advised her to concentrate on recovering in time for the '96 Games in Atlanta. But she confounded the experts by rowing to the bronze and becoming a true Canadian heroine.

Freestyle wrestler Jeff Thue (left, opposite) was ranked third in the world when he won the Olympic silver medal in the 130 kg class.

For Fréchette, the resolution was more emotionally painful and eventually more golden. Just a week before the Games, her fiancé committed suicide in their Montreal home. Then, in the compulsory portion of her event, a Brazilian judge inadvertently punched in the wrong score and could not correct it. The error cost Fréchette the gold medal and it was not until 16 months later, after inside manoeuvering by Canadian Olympic officials, that she was retroactively awarded a gold medal, which she shared with American Kristen Babb-Sprague, the original winner.

American runner Carl Lewis was a much-watched performer at Barcelona. The sprinter-jumper's star seemed to be on the wane after the American Olympic trials where, afflicted by a virus, he finished sixth in the 100 metres, in which he was two-time defending Olympic champion, and fourth in the 200 metres. But it's always dangerous to underestimate Lewis, who led a U.S. sweep of the Olympic men's long jump, edging world record holder Mike Powell by an inch and a quarter. Then he helped the U.S. 4 × 100-metre sprint team win, for his eighth Olympic gold medal, tied with American Ray Ewry for the second-highest total in Summer Games history.

Lewis's erstwhile rival, the ill-fated Ben Johnson, was back in Olympic competition after serving his two-year drug suspension — unfathomably, a few months later he would test positive a second time for steroids and incur a lifetime ban — but finished last in his 100-metre semi-final. Rarely has a last-place finisher received more public attention. Fellow sprinter Bruny Surin, who had displaced Johnson as Canada's fastest man, and cyclist Curt Harnett both complained that Johnson — who refused to stay at the athletes' village — was receiving unwarranted media coverage. Harnett himself won a bronze medal, which he called a disappointment because he had taken silver at Los Angeles. Surin was fourth in the 100 metres, won by Britain's Linford Christie, the new "world's fastest human."

Light welterweight boxer Mark Leduc was three-time national champion when he fought to a silver medal at the Barcelona Games.

Also on the rise was the Chinese team, which won 54 medals to finish fourth in the medal count behind the winning Unified Team, the United States, and Germany. But the Chinese performance raised eyebrows of suspicion. The suddenly dominant Chinese women's swimmers set world records in the 50-metre freestyle and 200-metre individual medley and an Olympic record in the 100-metre freestyle, inciting strong whispers about drug use.

For the Unified Team it was one final blaze of glory, led by gymnast Vitali Chtcherbo, who won six gold medals, and teammate Grigori Misioutine, who reaped two gold and three silver. Swimmer Alexandre Popov of the former Soviet team was the other big multiple winner with two gold and two silver. But the former Soviet athlete who was the biggest

lock for a medal came dead last. Defending Olympic pole vault champion Sergei Bubka, who had broken the world record 28 times, did not make any of his three jumps. Doubling Bubka's pain was the fact he was representing his native Ukraine for the first time at an Olympics.

Bubka's heartbreak paled beside that of American swimmer Ron Karnaugh, whose father died suddenly, just after taking photos of his son marching in the Opening Ceremonies. Less tragic was the broken leg incurred by Canadian sailor Murray McCaig, who was riding a bike in the athletes' village and was struck by a police car. Mark Leduc, among the least-known Canadian boxers before the Games, became synonymous with courage in taking a silver medal. He won his semi-final bout in the light welterweight division, despite boxing with a high fever caused by an abscessed mosquito bite and with a ruptured tendon in his right shoulder that made it painful to even raise his arm. He lost the final to Hector Vinent, one of seven Cubans to capture boxing gold. Canada also got a boxing bronze in the middleweight category from Chris Johnson.

Host Spain rose to the once-in-a-lifetime occasion with 22 medals, nearly matching its total 26 from all other Summer Games combined and more than tripling — from four to thirteen — its previous number of gold medals.

Canada also made its mark. A couple of Marks, actually. Swimmer Mark Tewksbury and sprinter Mark McKoy gave Canada a pair of gold medals that could not have come

Hurdler Mark McCoy gave Canada its first track and field gold since Duncan McNaughton's 1932 win in the high jump.

Mark Tewksbury tastes gold after his win in the 100 m backstroke, making him Canada's fifth Olympic champion in swimming since George Hodgson's double gold in 1912.

from more opposite personalities. Tewksbury, a 100-metre backstroke specialist, was as quietly underspoken as McKoy, the 110-metre hurdler, was controversial.

McKoy was born in Guyana but grew up in Toronto where he trained with the famous, and later infamous, Mazda Optimists Track Club at York University. A teammate and close friend of Ben Johnson, he was suspended when he left the 1988 Olympics before his scheduled appearance in the relay race. Later, he told the Dubin Inquiry into the use of drugs in competitive sport that he would never again compete for Canada because of what he considered the shabby treatment of Johnson. He also admitted that he had used steroids. He quit track and sold real estate, than ran as an independent when his suspension was lifted. He went to Wales to train with British hurdler Colin Jackson.

A couple of years later, McKoy competed for his adopted country of Austria, but at Barcelona, he was running under the maple leaf. McKoy beat Americans Tony Dees and Jack

Pierce to the tape to give Canada its first Olympic championship in a running event since the fabulous Percy Williams in 1928. At the finish line he and Jackson, who finished seventh, embraced. "I just forgot about the whole thing," McKoy said of Seoul. "I think the whole world of track and field needs to forget about it. It was a bad experience for track."

Like McKoy, Tewksbury outdistanced a couple of American challengers and climaxed a better Olympic year for his home town of Calgary than 1988, when it hosted the Games. "He exemplifies everything that is the Olympic ideal," Calgary Mayor Al Duerr said of the toothy-grinned Tewskbury. After getting a poor start, an immense obstacle in a 100-metre sprint, backstroker Tewskbury trailed Jeff Rouse with 10 metres to go, but bore down on the U.S. swimmer like a raptor on prey. He touched the wall in a new Olympic record (53.98 seconds).

Tewksbury also swam a leg on the 400-metre medley relay team which took bronze, Canada's only other race-swimming medal. Sylvie Fréchette and the Vilagos twins, Penny and Vicky, who had retired after failing to make the 1984 team but mounted a comeback in 1989, took silvers in synchronized swimming. McKoy's gold helped the Canadian track team enjoy its best showing since 1932, when added to Guillaume Leblanc's silver in the race walk and a bronze in the 3,000 metres from Victoria's Angela Chalmers. And 22-year-old Graham Hood of Burlington, perhaps using Barcelona as a stepping stone to Atlanta, finished ninth in the 1,500 metres, becoming the first Canadian male to make an Olympic 1,500-metre final since 1936.

Montreal judoka Nicolas Gill started competing at age six; 14 years later he took home a bronze from Barcelona.

But one Canadian team had no peers at these Barcelona Olympics, possibly, among Canada's team competitors, at *any* Olympics. This was the rowing team.

Prior to the Seoul Games, Canada had won a total of 19 Olympic sculling medals. But when disaster struck the rowers at the 1988 Games, with no medals and only one competitor, the men's heavy eights, reaching the finals, a catharsis followed. Rowing officials concluded that volunteers were interfering with training. It was time to get rid of the amateurs and hire professional coaching. The two pros who got the jobs were renowned Briton Mike Spracklen, in charge of the men's team centred in Victoria, and Al Morrow, new coach of the women's team in London, Ontario. The coaches made changes, doubling the number of weekly workouts and concentrating on fewer events. The payoff came early when the Canadian rowers captured four golds and a silver at the 1991 World Championships.

That success spilled over to Lake Banyoles near Barcelona, despite — or perhaps because of — Laumann's serious injury. On the middle Saturday of the Olympics, the women's fours team of Kirsten Barnes, Brenda Taylor, Jessica Monroe, and late substitute Kay Worthington took gold, followed 30 minutes later by a decisive win by the formidable pairs team of Marnie McBean and Kathleen Heddle. The next day, Laumann won her injury-defying bronze with a last-minute power surge. That performance, Marnie McBean later said, served as "an inspiration and motivator" to the other women.

Canada's rowers also took gold in the bigger boats, the eights, in both men's and women's. Darren Barber, Derek Porter, Andy Crosby, Mike Forgeron, Robert Marland, Michael Rascher, Bruce Robertson, John Wallace, and coxswain Terry Paul, edged a Romanian crew by 14/100ths of a second. The women's team included the gold medallist pairs and fours plus Megan Delehanty, Shannon Crawford, and coxswain Lesley Thompson. They simply out-powered all the other boats in the race, and the victory moved women's coach Al Morrow to speak the words that probably best summed up the feelings that these magnificent Canadian rowers had generated. "Everybody," Morrow said, "is in goo-goo land."

Gold was the name of the game for Canadian rowers in Barcelona, with first-place finishes in four events, three of them by women who became Canada's first-ever female gold medallists in rowing.

Profile

Silken Laumann

Bronze Medallist, rowing, 1984, 1992
Silver Medallist, 1996

The baby was so slim and delicate at birth that Sigitta Laumann named her new daughter Silken. Twenty-seven years later, Silken Laumann showed the world, not to mention her mother, that she was all power and pride, in a 78-day vortex that startled experts in sport and in medicine.

"She's so strong, so powerful, so willful," marvelled Sigitta after Silken overcame a potentially career-ending injury to win a bronze medal in the women's singles sculls at Barcelona. "I was thinking about Terry Fox and how determined he was. I think it's rather similar."

Sigitta was not the only one to make the comparison between the one-legged cancer victim who ran his way into a nation's mythology and Laumann, a victim of another kind. When she climbed into her boat for a training session in Essen, Germany, on May 16, 1992, the road that lay before Laumann appeared to be paved with nothing but gold. She was reigning world singles champion and the overwhelming favourite to win the Barcelona Olympics in less than three months time. She had considered retiring after a disappointing Seoul Olympics that reflected the problems of the entire rowing team, but rededicated herself to the sport and moved from her home town of Mississauga to Victoria to train under Mike Spracklen, the men's coach.

Her dream, however, turned into a nightmare that morning in Essen when a German pairs boat, rowed by eventual Barcelona silver medallists Peter Hoeltzenbein and Colin von Ettingshausen, sliced through her boat and into her calf. Displaced knots of muscle, tendons, and nerves had peeled away and dangled from her right calf, wood splinters were embedded in the flesh, and the broken right leg seemed almost incidental. The first person to glimpse Laumann's leg was one of the Germans who had rammed her, "and he passed out," recalled Gord Henry, manager of the Canadian rowing delegation. "The second guy was trying to hold her up so she wouldn't slide into the water, and he didn't see the leg until the rescue boat took her away. Then he passed out too."

As soon as her pain abated even slightly, Laumann began exercising in her hospital bed: working the upper body with barbells, stretching the unaffected leg. She had emotional and physical support from her boyfriend and future husband, John Wallace, a member of the men's heavy eights team. "I don't think I ever gave up completely," said Laumann of those early days. "The doctors were saying immediately after it happened that it was so serious that there was no way, and I had to accept that. But a little part of me was saying, 'Maybe I can do it'."

That little part kept growing. She had five reconstructive surgeries, with a sixth reserved until after the Olympics. She was first in a wheelchair, then on crutches, then walked with the aid of a cane and a brace, but she continued to work out. "For me, that was a form of therapy," she explained.

When Laumann was finally able to climb into a rowing shell, her technique, despite — or perhaps because of — the injury, seemed to be improved. She had gained speed and confidence.

Eventually, with eyebrows raised by everyone except those closest to her, Laumann declared herself ready for Barcelona. She compared herself to an actress heading into a big play without all her lines memorized, but was determined to compete. "I'm not going to set any expectations for myself other than just racing really well," she said. "The last thing I want to do is be disappointed after all the positive things that have happened."

On July 28, she inched up to the starting line and successfully completed the qualifying heat of the Olympic 2,000-metre singles event. Three days later, she won her semi-final. An enraptured nation awakened three hours before dawn to watch the live telecast of the women's final. Romania's Elisabeta Lipa and Belgium's Annelies Bredael pulled away by the halfway point, leaving Laumann and American Ann Marden to stroke it out for the bronze. Marden went ahead with 500 metres to go, but by upping her pace to an astonishing 38 strokes per minute through the final 200 metres, Laumann passed Marden and came across the finish line as bronze medallist.

"At no time, through all of these weeks, did I ever think I'd end up with a medal," said the ecstatic Laumann. "But when the crunch came near the finish, I knew I didn't want to come fourth."

Silken Laumann's grit and determination symbolize the Olympic ideal for millions of admirers around the world.

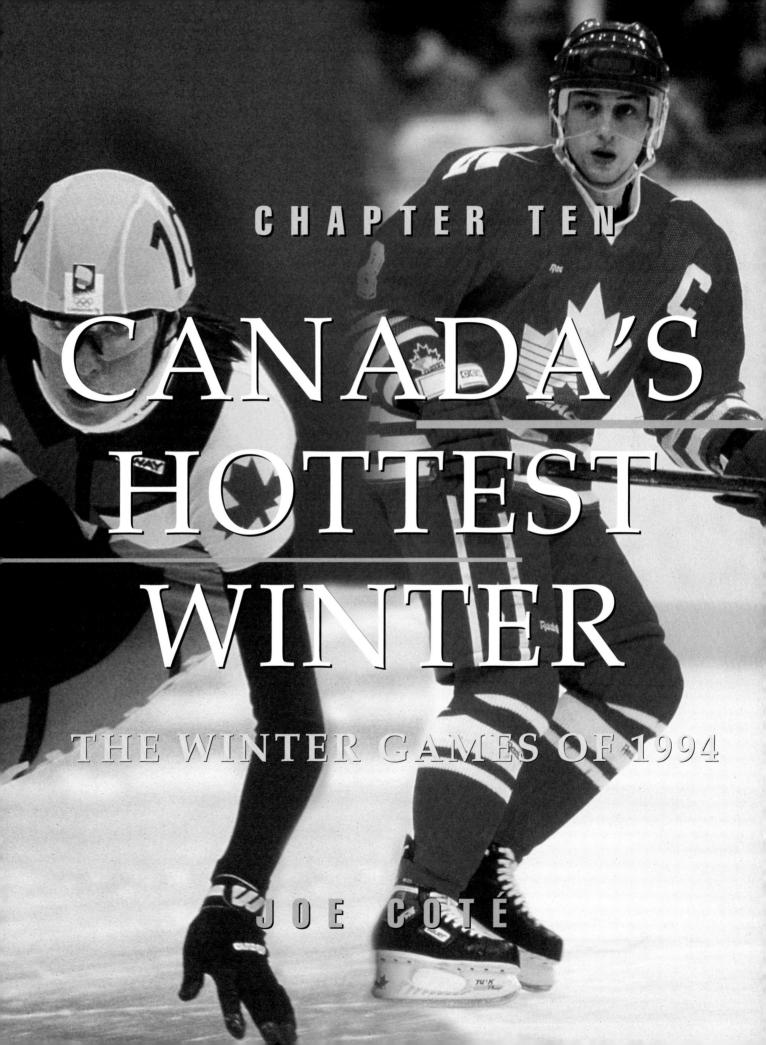

CHAPTER TEN

CANADA'S HOTTEST WINTER

THE WINTER GAMES OF 1994

JOE COTÉ

B eep, beep, beep.

The electronic signal in the start-house a kilometre up Kvitfjell mountain sounded the beat as Edi Podivinski steadied himself for his downhill run. Suddenly the 22-year-old racer from Edmonton lunged forward. His shins kicked open the timer wand. The clock started. Podivinski attacked the course in a run that was to signal something splendid for Canada over the next fortnight of the Winter Olympics in the frigid, snow-packed, lovely Norwegian town of Lillehammer.

Just the night before, Canadians in black "Mountie"-style hats and blazing red cloaks had strode confidently into the Olympic Stadium — a display of what was perhaps Canada's best winter team ever. One hundred and four young Canadians had come to compete, and they brought with them more than hope and crossed fingers. Finally, if all the signs were right, Canada had assembled a corps of athletes who could skate and ski, shoot and stickhandle, jump and spin with the best in the world. Kurt Browning, who carried Canada's flag on opening night, belonged in the world-class category. So did speed-skater Susan Auch and aerialist Jean-Luc Brassard and biathlon specialist Myriam Bédard. And there were others in the Canadian contingent who had an authentic shot at a medal.

Canadian spectators at Lillehammer were treated to the best performance ever by a Canadian Winter Olympics team— three gold medals, six silver, and four bronze. A surprise bronze came from downhiller Edi Podivinski (opposite).

But few thought Edi Podivinski was necessarily among this élite group.

Our Crazy Canuck ski team of the 1970s and 1980s had gone soft. At least the men's team had. Wins on the World Cup circuit were rare, so it was a welcome surprise when the latest "Pod" opened Canada's medal account with a brave dash down the icy pitch just north of Lillehammer. Edi Podivinski's name brought back memories of Steve Podborski, the world champion of the early 1980s, when Canada's men's downhill team ruled the runs. But Edi was a different kind of downhiller. In the years before the Winter Games of 1994, he had enjoyed one party and one tum-

Kurt Browning salutes the crowd during his final Olympic performance, and teammate Elvis Stojko, a 1994 silver medallist, displays the aggressive stance that marks his controversial skating style. Opposite: Pairs skaters Isabelle Brasseur and Lloyd Eisler were crowd pleasers at Lillehammer, where they won a bronze medal.

ble too many. Edi decided that reform was the better route to follow. He changed his lifestyle off the *piste* and plunged into a fitness campaign. It paid off, not by miles but by millimetres, and that was all he needed. Downhillers, after all, beat each other by little more than the width of a ski pole after two minutes of near reckless descent. On that first of many stunningly bright mornings, Podivinski's route down Kvitfjell mountain was just a fingertip faster than all but two other racers. The Pod had a bronze, earned with heart and guts, and early-to-bed nights.

Two days later, Podivinski and teammate Cary Mullen had near misses, finishing fifth and fourth in the combined downhill. On the women's team, surprisingly, the best prospects did not deliver. Kate Pace of North Bay was the reigning world downhill champion, and Kerrin Lee-Gartner had taken Olympic gold in the Super G at Albertville two years earlier. Both managed top ten finishes on the Kvitfjell, but the podium eluded them.

Narrowly missing victory turned out to be Kurt Browning's story too. Four world titles and a bust at Albertville had set up the charismatic skater from Caroline, Alberta, for a second chance at a gold medal. This time there were no back problems to bedevil him, but there were old rivals returned from the pros, the American Brian Boitano and the Ukrainian Viktor Petrenko. Most of all there was Browning's brilliant teammate Elvis Stojko, a flat-out jumping machine who was starting to put some soul into his proven acrobatics. Canada's one-two punch looked hard to beat.

But Browning's chances for gold tumbled fast and early in his short program. Just seconds into the routine, he couldn't land a triple flip. That slip put him out of contention for a medal. Gallantly, Browning came back two nights later in his long program and, as far as his fans were concerned, skated like a dream to music from *Casablanca*, playing Humphrey Bogart in a

white dinner jacket. He didn't move the judges to ecstasy — they placed Browning in a final seventh place — but he rescued himself from embarrassment.

Into the breach left by Browning skated — or, maybe more accurately, catapulted — Elvis Stojko. Stojko was the odd man out in the world of figure skating, a leather-and-studs guy rather than a blouse-and-tuxedo artiste. Stojko held a black belt in karate, and he brought the same athletic intensity to his figure skating. It had taken a long time for the judges to adjust to Stojko's original and aggressive style, but at Lillehammer they understood enough of his artistry to award him a silver medal.

In pairs skating, the reigning world champions, Lloyd Eisler and Isabelle Brasseur, had to face the return of the dazzling Olympic champions from Calgary '88, Russians Yekaterina Gordeeva and Sergey Grinkov, now matured and married and still a wonder to watch. The table was set for a feast of skating, until Brasseur was injured during practice. She came down hard from one of Eisler's ceiling-high throws, crashed into his chest, and cracked a rib. In spite of her pain, the two thrilled the crowd at Hamar, and the judges rewarded them with the bronze medal. The pair accepted it in the most dramatic fashion at the awards ceremony, when Eisler, the rangy part-time hockey player, spun across the ice with the petite Brasseur perched on his shoulder.

Josée Chouinard gamely skated in the long shadow cast over the 1994 Games by the notorious Nancy Kerrigan-Tonya Harding affair.

Josée Chouinard's troubles came from another quarter. The Lillehammer Games were at times an unhappy sideshow to the bizarre duel between the two American skaters, Nancy Kerrigan and Tonya Harding. Kerrigan had been clubbed in the knee just before the American National Championships a couple of months earlier, and Harding may have known a little too much about the attack. For Chouinard, Kerrigan was a problem simply because she skated so superbly and ended up with the silver medal. Harding presented Chouinard with a hazard of a different and more immediate sort. Just as Harding, who skated without much finesse throughout the competition, launched into her long program, she suddenly, perversely, pulled up. She whined to the judges that she'd broken a lace on one of her strangely battered boots. She was

awarded a chance to regroup and skate again. Meanwhile the next scheduled skater was rushed on to the ice without proper time to warm up physically or psychologically. Who was this unlucky next skater? She was Canada's Josée Chouinard, who promptly crashed out of medal competition with a couple of unfortunate falls. Years of preparation by Chouinard had been skewed by the politics and pettiness of another skater.

Over at the Viking Ship, the arena that resembled an overturned rowboat, Canada was about to get back into speed-skating. It had been 18 years since a Canadian woman last won a medal in long track, and Susan Auch of Winnipeg had set

Susan Auch was the first Canadian woman to take home an individual speed-skating medal since Cathy Priestner's silver in 1976.

herself a punishing regimen to regain her country's reputation. Auch began her career on the speed teams, then switched to long track, taking on a training program of winters at the rink and summers on a bike to whip herself into shape. In the 500 metres at Lillehammer, she was up against the incomparable American, Bonnie Blair, and for a few glorious moments, after an extraordinarily fast start, it looked as if Auch might take the measure of Blair. But at the bell, Auch slipped back ever so slightly, just enough to let Blair take gold by an eyebrow. It was silver for Auch.

The other brand of speed-skating, short-track, is the roller derby of Olympic events. To be sure, there are rules: no touching the other skaters, no crossing another skater's line. But almost everything else about the sport — the multi-coloured body suits, flashing steel blades, pumping arms, team tactics – suggest something more indecorous. Short-track is a relatively recent Olympic sport — the Lillehammer Games represented short-track's third Games appearance —but Canada had already made itself a short-track power.

Short-track speed-skaters Christine Boudrias and Isabelle Charest were members of the relay team that was eventually awarded silver.

The Canadian women's team had captured the gold medal at Albertville two years earlier, and the big four — Nathalie Lambert, Sylvie Daigle, Christine Boudrias, and Isabelle Charest — shaped up as medal winners at Lillehammer. But not, as it turned out, the gold. In the 3,000-metre relay, trouble came with an awkward tag that dropped the Canadians into a final third place. When the Chinese skaters, who finished ahead of the Canadians, were disqualified on a late call of interference, Canada moved up to silver.

A similar piece of twisted fate happened to short-track skater Marc Gagnon. The race was the 1,000 metres, and in the semi-finals, which turned into a shambles, Gagnon stumbled, fell, and momentarily lost his chance to compete in the finals. But did that cost him a chance at a medal? Not in the crazy world of short-track. Gagnon skated in the B final and won it. In the A final for the medals, two of the four skaters found themselves disqualified for various transgressions, and that series of events moved Gagnon up a couple of notches to bronze medal status.

Marc Gagnon left Lillehammer with a bronze for his short-track performance.

Nathalie Lambert, already toting a medal from the 3,000-metre relay, approached the 1,000-metre singles with a certain amount of trepidation. She was hurting badly from an earlier collision, and deciding she couldn't gamble on possessing the strength for a late surge, she came out fast and set the early pace. Her hope was to hold the lead from start to finish. She almost succeeded. She roared down the stretch with two Korean skaters, and when the three hit the finish line, Lambert was in the middle, a stride behind one Korean, a stride ahead of the other. She got silver.

If short-track skating is public and fractious, then the biathlon is solitary and contemplative. The competitor skis swiftly, and alone, from target to target and must remain sufficiently focused and calm to fire off a required number of rifle shots at each target. For some reason, even though Canada has plenty of areas

where the sport can be learned and practised, the biathlon has never caught on. Which is where Myriam Bédard comes in. Bédard learned marksmanship as a teenager in the army cadets, then added the skiing skills. Mental and physical toughness completed the package, and Bédard got so proficient at her lonely and demanding sport that she took a bronze medal at Albertville.

That victory made Bédard a popular favourite in Lillehammer, and in the first competition, the 15 kilometres, she delivered the goods. Starting virtually at the end of the field, number 67 out of the 70 competitors, she swept through the field with a 46-second margin of victory, missing only two of the twenty required targets. That gave her one gold medal, and in the 7.5 kilometres, she went for a second. This time, heading into the final hill, she seemed too far back to win. It was little wonder she trailed — as Bédard was to discover days later, she was wearing mismatched skis, one waxed for extreme cold, the other for milder conditions. Still, despite this bizarre handicap, she turned on a remarkable push down the home stretch and recorded a time that stood up as the best in the competition by a single second over the second-place finisher. That gave Bédard two biathlon golds, the only Canadian apart from speed-skater Gaëtan Boucher to produce a double gold at a Winter Olympics.

Freestyle skiing is even more recent to the Winter Olympics than short-track skating. Lillehammer was only the second Olympics that listed the sport as a medal event, but Canada had already established its authority in the sport. The Canadian aces gloried in the name of the Quebec Air Force, and its main man was an audacious fellow, Jean-Luc Brassard of Grand-Ile, Quebec, who learned his tricks skiing down a homemade ramp from the eavestrough of the family home beside the St. Lawrence River. That's where he began to absorb the spins and flips and other aerial moves with exotic names — "the Iron Cross-Cossack Combination" — that are the essence of the sport. Brassard's older mentor was Edgar Grospiron of France, the man known as "Crazy Eddie." It was Grospiron who took the gold in the men's moguls at Albertville, to Brassard's seventh place, and it was Grospiron whom Brassard set out to defeat at Lillehammer. In the crunch, Brassard pulled off a perfect run — fast, dazzling, including the Iron Cross-Cossack Combination — and he drew enough points from the judges to place him ahead of his old mentor. In fact, Grospiron fell into third place, and the young Canadian took the gold.

The other members of the Quebec Air Force — Philippe LaRoche, a two-time world champion and gold medallist at Albertville, and Lloyd Langlois, the reigning

Shooting and Nordic skiing are twinned in the biathlon—the event that belongs to Myriam Bédard after her double gold wins at Lillehammer.

world champion — got into the act when the men's aerials were staged a week after Brassard's moguls win. The credentials of LaRoche and Langlois qualified them as favourites for Olympic medals. But nobody reckoned with the old-timer in the field, Switzerland's Sonny Schoenbaechler, who announced the Olympic competition was his farewell to the sport. Some farewell. After the judges studied all the competitors and rated the grace and artistry of their twisting back flips and somersaults, they posted the order of finish this way: Schoenbaechler, LaRoche, and Langlois. That added up to two more medals for Canada, though neither was the hoped-for gold.

Going into Lillehammer, the last time Canada had won a gold medal in hockey, Canadians were at war in Korea, the United States liked Ike, the Beatles were short-haired grade-school kids, and Roger Bannister still hadn't cracked the four-minute mark. The Edmonton Mercurys had gone undefeated at the Oslo Games of 1952. By 1994, the best of the Russian and Czechs were now in the NHL, and the struggling new nations of Eastern Europe couldn't afford to pamper their hockey teams. At the same time, Canada was building a slick, quick team of its own. It began with a nice balance of fresh young faces and reasonably seasoned pros, and as the Games came closer, the Canadians added

"Quebec Air Force" freestylers Philippe LaRoche and Lloyd Langlois celebrate their second- and third-place wins. Opposite: Gold medallist Jean-Luc Brassard shows off the flashy moves that make up freestyle skiing.

such authentic stars as Petr Nedved, the classy scorer who was sitting out the season over a contract dispute with the Vancouver Canucks, and Paul Kariya, the best player in U.S. college hockey and a number four pick in the NHL draft. With these guys, with steady Corey Hirsch in goal, with a reasonable amount of punch in the offence and unremitting toughness on the defence, Canada ran undefeated through the opening round robin with respectable wins over Italy, France, Slovakia, and Sweden, and a tie against the United States.

On the eve of the quarter-final match-up against the Czech Republic, Myriam Bédard dropped in on the team for a morale booster. She took along her gold medal

from the 15-kilometre biathlon. She showed the medal to the hockey team, told them what it took to win gold, spoke of working to make a dream come true.

The next day the Canadians struggled but didn't give up, bent but didn't break. The game, at 2–2, went into overtime. This was the kind of situation when a weaker Canadian team would go into a folding act. Not this time. At the five-minute mark, on a power play, Paul Kariya grabbed a rebound and fired it into the Czech net.

Two days later, in the semi-finals against Finland, Canada fell behind 2–0. Again it looked like a signal for a Canadian collapse. Again the team showed stronger stuff. Canada reeled off five straight goals until Finland scored a mean-ingless final-seconds marker. It was 5–3, and Canada was going for gold against the Swedes.

This, as it turned out, was a game for the ages. For starters, it produced great

Swedish player Svensson puts one past Canadian goalie Corey Hirsch in the final-game shootout that cost Canada the gold medal.

hockey, elegant Swedish passing against gritty Canadian checking, Swedish finesse versus Canadian determination. Finesse seemed to have the edge. The Swedes out-shot Canada in regulation time, 42–21. But Corey Hirsch's stubborn goaltending and the overall Canadian fortitude — these players weren't quitters — sent the game into a 2–2 overtime.

Then, with no goals in the overtime, the infamous shoot-out got under way. According to the rules, which struck hockey purists as just this side of crazy, each team named five shooters. These 10 players alternated with shots on the opposing goalie. Whoever scored the most goals on the fewest shots won. If things were all tied after the first shoot-around, then different shooters took their turns with one significant difference: the first team to score, as long as the other team had stayed scoreless on the same number of shots, emerged as the winner.

Complex? Yes. Ridiculous? For sure. But a prescription for tremendous excitement? Absolutely, right up there with the eighth game in the 1972 Canada-Russia series, except there was no Paul Henderson this time.

The two teams went through the first run of five shooters and finished in a stalemate. Now it was sudden death. The first shooter for each team failed to score. Then Sweden broke the ice when Peter Forsberg slipped a backhand under Corey Hirsch's glove. Paul Kariya was next up for Canada. He went with a high wrister, the same sort of shot he'd scored on earlier. But this time the Swedish goalie, Tommy Salo, blocked the puck with his leg pad. The game was over, and it was silver for Canada.

Until Lillehammer, the highest medal total that Canada had accumulated was seven at Lake Placid in 1932 and the same at Albertville in 1992. The 1994 athletes had almost doubled those figures. Thirteen medals in all, three gold, six silver, four bronze. In total medals, that tied Canada with the United States behind only four countries. The fortnight at Lillehammer had established these 104 young athletes as the finest Canadian Olympic Winter Team in the country's history.

Profile

Myriam Bédard

BRONZE MEDALLIST 1992;
DOUBLE GOLD MEDALLIST, BIATHLON, 1994

Growing up in L'Ancienne-Lorette in the suburbs of Quebec City, Myriam Bédard showed herself to be a natural-born athlete from childhood. She excelled at gymnastics, figure skating, and basketball. There was just one problem; classes and clubs for most sports proved an expensive proposition for Bédard's dad, an electrician with a wife and four kids. As an alternative, Bédard followed the pattern of her friends: she joined the army cadets. That move led her, willy nilly, into the odd and lonely sport of the biathlon.

Bédard was 15, in her first year at the Val-Cartier cadet camp, when she learned to shoot. Again, she was a natural. Still it was a long leap to participating on Val-Cartier's biathlon team, because Bédard didn't know how to ski. Undeterred, she borrowed a set of skis, stuffed tissue into an out-sized pair of men's ski boots, and helped her team to victory in a relay event.

That summer, already committed to the biathlon, she splurged her savings on her own cross-country skis. She went for the whole package, membership in a ski club, lessons on the hills. At the same time, she stepped up her biathlon competition. One drawback was the rifle she used, a heavy and ancient weapon that almost outweighed its owner. The problem was solved in typical forthright Bédard fashion. A customer in a store where Bédard worked part-time asked about her plans for life. "I'm going to be a champion," the perky Bédard answered. The charmed customer kicked in enough money to buy a new rifle.

At 17, Bédard captured the Canadian Junior Biathlon Championship, then became the first Canadian to win a World Cup event. She kept moving forward. When she was 21, she took two golds, two silvers, and a bronze on the World Cup circuit, finishing second overall on the year. It was the highest ranking ever achieved by a North American.

Bédard's technique was unusual. When other skiers reach the target range, they stop to steady their breathing after the gruelling stretch of skiing. Bédard developed a more fluid form, moving from skiing to shooting without the usual pause. The technique, along with her remarkable rifle accuracy, came from uncommon commitment and the joy she took in her sport's loneliness. She trained ferociously and developed an aerobic capacity that measured at an astounding 75. By contrast, a fit hockey player manages something in the neighbourhood of 55.

Bédard's single-mindedness, which was great for competition, got her in trouble with her sport's officials. Biathlon Canada wanted a say in her training and sponsorships. Bédard insisted on striking her own deals. That bit of insubordination led Biathlon Canada to ground Bédard for one whole season.

The bad blood from that episode never quite cleared, and Bédard went her own determined way in seeking financial support. It takes plenty, about $250,000, to maintain a biathlon athlete in training and competition the year round. At one point, to keep going, Bédard ran her fingers through the entire Quebec City phone book dialling potential sponsors. As usual with Bédard, the determination eventually paid off in backing.

Bédard's charms with potential sponsors didn't seem to work with coaches. She claimed that she couldn't work with Biathlon Canada's coaches. So she developed her own training routines and dispensed with coaching pep talks. "The inspiration," she said, "must come from the heart."

Eventually rumours circulated that Bédard had a mystery trainer. That got her in deeper trouble with Biathlon Canada, and a couple of years went by before the mystery man was revealed as Steffen Thierfelder, a European biathlon specialist who faxed and phoned Bédard with tips and training schedules. None of this endeared her to Canadian officials, but it paid off in wins in competition.

Bédard's fanatical training, her unorthodox methods, her cautions to her parents that they must never shout distracting cheers for her during competition all contributed to two gold medals in Lillehammer. First came the win in the 15 kilometres when she blew away the opposition, then the thrilling and narrow victory in the 7.5 kilometres, when she prevailed over both the other competitors and her own mismatched skis. It was the ultimate double triumph for the obstinate young women whom her parents used to call "*tête de cochon.*"

CHAPTER ELEVEN

GUTS and GLORY in ATLANTA

THE SUMMER GAMES OF 1996

JACK & BRAD BATTEN

DID CANADIANS EXPECT TO HAVE IT THIS GOOD? TWENTY-TWO MEDALS. Three gold, eleven silver, eight bronze. Eleventh overall in medal standings. Even though Canadian athletes and their fans back home approached Atlanta with an optimism that owed its origins to the splendid showing four years earlier in Barcelona, the results of the Centennial Games still had the power to amaze. Besides the medals, there was a record time in the centrepiece event of track and field. And there were heroes and heroines almost too numerous to mention. This was in the end an Olympics for Canada to cherish.

Some 10,000 athletes from over 200 nations gathered in Atlanta for the Centennial Olympic Games.

If we had high expectations of the 1996 Summer Games in Atlanta, our enthusiasm was understandable. After all, a decade ago, we had expected them to be *our* Olympics, expected that they would take place on Canadian soil, that the host city of the Centennial Olympiad would be our very own Toronto. But it didn't pan out that way.

Paul Henderson tried his mightiest. A former Olympic yachtsman, the third generation of his family to run a prosperous Toronto industrial plumbing business, Henderson conceived and drove the campaign to bring the 1996 Games to Toronto. "I love my city," Henderson said, "and I'm an Olympian." These were worthy credentials, and Henderson and much of the rest of Canada thought that they, along with a sensible, low-key, five-year, $16-million selling program, would persuade the International Olympic Committee to look fondly on Toronto's bid for the Games. Alas for Henderson, he was sandbagged on two fronts: at home and in Atlanta, Georgia.

The trouble domestically wasn't that Toronto politicians failed to support Henderson; Toronto City Council ultimately voted 13-5 in favour of the bid. The trouble was that the vote came reluctantly and late, after a rancorous debate in which left-wing council members argued that Olympic funding would be better spent in addressing Toronto's social problems, like a shortage of affordable housing and declining public services. This approach was echoed by a vocal and well-organized anti-Olympic lobbying group called the Bread Not Circuses Coalition. The combination of tardy official backing together with the strength of the local forces opposed to the Games had an unsettling impact on the IOC.

Meanwhile, Atlanta, Toronto's chief rival for the Games, was bragging that every state and municipal authority in all of Georgia had approved legislation on *its* bid without a single murmur of dissension. Atlanta boasted. And Atlanta prevaricated: in its submission to the IOC, it fudged the not-so-inconsequential fact that the Games would take place during the city's most oppressive weather, in temperatures above 30 degrees Celsius and in suffocating humidity. Atlanta was aggressive in making its case. It rode over rumours, rampant but never quite proven, that it helped things along by spreading largesse among the 88 voting members of the IOC. And in the end, bragging, prevaricating, aggressive Atlanta got the votes and got the Games.

But if Canadians were disappointed in their dreams of playing host to the Olympics, they had a fall-back position. They would invest their hopes in the country's athletes. As 1996 drew closer, it seemed clear to Canada that it had a strong cycling team, an even stronger rowing team, and, in Donovan Bailey and Bruny

Atlanta's Opening Ceremonies were as lavish and spectacular as viewers have come to expect of Games held in the United States.

Surin, the top two finishers in the 1995 World Championship 100-metre sprint. Canadians expected all of them, and other athletes, too, to bring home medals from Atlanta. Brian Williams, the lead CBC-TV host at the Games, predicted that Canada would win 21 medals, eight of them gold. Compared with other prognosticators, Williams had come down on the conservative side. His CBC-TV co-host, Ron McLean, figured on 30 medals for Canada, including 10 gold. His gung-ho estimate seemed to reflect the expectations of most Canadians.

All of which meant that many of the early results from Atlanta fell into the category of shocked disillusionment. Canadian athletes who had seemed surefire prospects tumbled out of contention, and Canada's hopes began to falter.

Take the case of Anne Montminy. She was the spunky diver from Montreal, rated fourth best in the world in the 10-metre platform event. A cinch at least to make the Olympic finals, right? Wrong. In the preliminaries, Montminy made, in her own words, "pretty much the four worst dives I've done in six months." She finished twenty-fourth. Only the best 18 divers advanced. So much for the peak of Montminy's distinguished diving career. "I just had a bad day," she said.

The 305-member Canadian Olympic Team marches behind their flag-bearer, runner Charmaine Crooks.

She had a bad day? Nicolas Gill had a bad five seconds. Linda Jackson had a worse split second. These were heartbreakers.

Gill, a judo competitor from Montreal, was perhaps the victim of misplaced ambition. At the 1992 Olympics, he stunned the judo world by winning an unexpected bronze medal in the 86-kilogram middleweight class. By the '96 Games, his natural weight was about nine kilograms above the 86-kilo limit, but rather than competing in the 95-kilogram half-heavyweight class, he insisted on dieting and training down to the lower division. Why? Because the 86-kilo event was rightly regarded as the toughest in all of judo, and Gill craved the challenge. So it was that, at less than his optimum strength, he was flattened by Mark Huizinga of the Netherlands a mere five seconds into their match. Gill ended up in a disappointing seventh place.

Linda Jackson of Ottawa came a cropper in the cycling road race, which stretched more than 100 kilometres through Atlanta's overheated streets. Jackson, 37, had been pointing to this event with high purposefulness ever since the day three

Double bronze medallist Clara Hughes embraces cycling teammate Linda Jackson, who was forced to leave the road race after an accident.

Curtis Myden went to Atlanta as the 1995 Canadian champion at the 200 m and 400 m individual medley and won bronze in both. Opposite: Marianne Limpert stroked to silver in the 200 m individual medley at the Georgia Tech Aquatic Centre.

years earlier when she gave up a six-figure job as a California investment banker to work full-time on her cycling. But five minutes into the Atlanta race, cyclists immediately in front of Jackson skidded into a sickening crash. Jackson, braking to avoid the wreckage of bikes and riders, flew over her handlebars and cracked into a mailbox. She came away from the mêlée with injuries to the tendons and muscles of her right arm. The injuries put her out of the race, all of her sacrifice and dedication gone for nothing in a brief moment of horrendously bad luck.

At least Gill and Jackson had a small shot at competing in their events. James Ransom had barely that, and the blame for his misfortune fell squarely on the Atlanta organizers. Ransom was a fencer from Nepean, Ontario, and on the morning of his bout against the American Michael Marx in the individual épée, a Games bus driver, assigned to ferry Ransom to his match, drove him to the wrong venue, then got lost, then got stuck in traffic. Ransom arrived minutes before his match, giving him no time to warm up. "Marx was feeling me out," Ransom said after the bout, "but as soon as he realized I couldn't move, it was all over." Ransom lost 15-8, the victim of a Games transportation system that kept breaking down.

Especially in the opening week, much of Atlanta's infrastructure seemed not to be operating on all cylinders. Or any cylinders at all. Buses ran late and in the wrong

196

Derek Porter (above) was a member of the gold medal-winning men's eights rowing team in Barcelona in 1992. Below: Porter shows off his 1996 silver medal in the single sculls to his mother.

directions. The computer system failed to generate the promised information to fans and the media. And much of the Olympic ambience, with its Coca-Cola Olympic City, its Swatch Pavilion, and its Nike Park, had borrowed from the tackiest side of capitalism. "Other Olympic cities decided they weren't going to turn the Games into a carnival," said Dick Pound, an IOC vice-president from Canada. "For Atlanta, it's a missed opportunity." As if to underscore the apparent deterioration in Olympic standards and values, it was in the site most devoted to commerce where ghastly tragedy befell the 1996 Games. It was in Centennial Park, a non-secured showplace for all

that was gaudy, that the infamous pipe bomb accounted for two deaths in Atlanta.

For Canada, as some athletes who carried their country's greatest hopes came to grief in crazy circumstances—Gill, Jackson—others of whom less was expected emerged from nowhere to begin the Canadian claim on medals. Clara Hughes, for example. She was a 23-year-old cyclist from Winnipeg who

triumphed in the very road race that shattered Linda Jackson. Hughes managed to skirt the crash of bikes, survive the oppressive heat, persist through the sudden rain that hit midway through the race, and pedal furiously to a bronze medal. By the standards of her event, Hughes was a comparative child—"I'm still fairly immature in my cycling career," she admitted—but it was young Clara who captured the first medal ever won by a Canadian woman in Olympic cycling.

A similar turn of events happened in women's swimming, a Canadian underdog came through when a teammate was unable to deliver the goods. Joanne Malar of Hamilton entered the Olympics as a popular favourite for medals in the individual medley events. But the enormous and probably unfair expectations heaped on her proved too heavy a load—nor was she helped by a low-iron blood condition that slowed down her recovery rate between races—and she failed to produce

Marnie McBean and Kathleen Heddle became Canada's first triple gold medallists in rowing.

medals in the 400-metre individual medley or the 200-metre IM. But the redoubtable Marianne Limpert of Fredericton picked up the slack. "I could lie back quietly while [Joanne] got all the attention," Limpert explained. She proceeded to chalk up a personal best time in the 200-metre IM final, losing only to Ireland's Michelle Smith, the swimming surprise of the entire Games, and capturing a silver medal for Canada.

It was in the individual medley events that a Canadian man made his mark in the pool. Curtis Myden, a soft-spoken 22-year-old student from the University of Calgary, set a Canadian record in the 400-metre IM final and beat every swimmer except the two acknowledged American stars of the event, Tom Dolan and Eric Namesnik. That gave Myden one bronze medal. In the 200-metre IM final, he set another Canadian record and finished behind Hungary's Attila Czene, who established an Olympic record, and Finland's world record holder Jani Sievenen. That gave Myden two bronze medals.

Now the medals were starting to pile up for the Canadians—and it may have had something to do with water. Limpert and Myden triumphed *in* the water, and on the second Saturday of the Games, our rowers did the same thing *on* the water, specifically Lake Lanier, the lovely venue for rowers and paddlers that had been created by damming the Chattahoochie River. Canada entered ten boats, eight of them reached the finals, none finished worse than seventh, and six took medals. Could Canadians have expected more?

Well, being greedy about it, maybe a little more. Maybe a gold for the great and gallant Silken Laumann in the single sculls. She settled for silver when Ekaterina Khodotovich of Belarus nipped to the wire 0:2.94 in front of Laumann after a thrilling duel over the final quarter. No regrets, Laumann said afterwards.

Rower Silken Laumann retained her hold on Canadians' hearts with her silver medal performance.

Unfinished business, Derek Porter of Victoria implied after he got *his* silver in the men's singles sculls. He lost by 2.6 seconds in the final to Xeno Mueller of Switzerland. Mueller, an erratic racer, a guy Porter had frequently beaten in the past, was decidedly an upset winner, and Porter—intelligent, steady, dedicated—left the impression

that he just might take more time out from his chiropractic studies over the next four years to prepare for gold in Sydney in 2000.

Marnie McBean and Kathleen Heddle got their third rowing gold in Atlanta. McBean of Toronto (she's the ebullient one) and Heddle of Vancouver (she's the restrained one) had won gold medals in the pairs and in the eights at Barcelona. On Lake Lanier, they were rowing the double sculls. With the pairs, each pulled on one oar, with the doubles each pulled on two oars, and the switch was rather like moving from softball to baseball—and playing in the World Series. No easy feat.

In their gold medal race, McBean and Heddle zipped to an early lead, then staved off two challenges from the Netherlands boat. Each time the Dutch pair drew close, McBean called for an extra push. The Dutch grew disheartened, but in the last few metres the Chinese boat came relentlessly at the Canadians. "I felt like we were just hanging on," McBean said.

All of Canada's medal winners in rowing had amazing stories of courage to tell— the bronze-winning women's quads, the silver-winning men's lightweight fours, and the others—but the women's eights qualified as the grandest surprise among the Canadians. Sure, they were the defending champs, winners of the gold in Barcelona. But only one of the eight women who rowed in '92 remained in '96, and boats from at least two nations, Romania and the United States, shaped up as superior. Nevertheless, driven and cajoled by the brilliant cox Lesley Thompson, the women

Caroline Brunet's rise to a silver medal in Atlanta's 500 m individual kayak race was a steady one: she was 13th in Seoul (1988) and seventh in Barcelona (1992).

Canadian heavyweight silver
medallist David Defiagbon
grimaces after he receives
a "low blow" from French
boxer Christophe Mendy.
Bottom: Guivi Sissaouri
brought home Canada's tenth
wrestling medal since 1908.

surged to a silver medal, behind Romania and a brave flick of the oars in front of third-place Belarus.

Brian Walton, a skinny 30-year-old from North Delta, B.C., displayed courage to burn in the cycling points event. This is a bizarre and supremely taxing competition that requires 28 riders to storm 160 laps—or about 40 kilometres—around the velodrome track with an all-out sprint every eight laps. At one stage of the race, Walton slipped an entire lap behind the leaders and appeared to be conclusively out of medal contention. But he put extraordinary demands on his body to overtake the riders in front. "I was suffering out there," Walton confessed afterwards. "I was dying."

Not quite. His magnificent comeback took him past every rider but one—the gold medallist Silvio Martinello of Italy—and the inspired Walton grabbed the silver. Inspiration indeed. Curt Harnett, the veteran cyclist and double Olympic medallist from Thunder Bay, Ontario, was so moved by Walton's performance—"It was the most awesome thing I've ever seen," he said—that minutes after Walton's race ended, Harnett wheeled on to the velodrome track and raced to his third medal, a bronze, in the sprint event.

Canada could hardly have anticipated that its athletes would produce medals in beach volleyball or mountain cycling: the Atlanta Games represented the first time the two sports had ever been Olympic medal events. Nevertheless, John Child and Mark Heese, a couple of Toronto guys who practised in a converted warehouse when no outdoor sand was available, volleyed their way to a bronze medal. And in the mountain bike race, an event that took competitors three laps around a 10.65 kilometre route through fields and forest trails on an overall climb of 270 metres, a plucky North Vancouver cyclist named Alison Sydor rode to a marvelous silver on a day that, she said, found her at less than her peak form.

Controversial judging in a bout against Bulgarian lightweight Tontcho Tontchev cost national champion boxer Mike Strange (left) a shot at a medal.

Canadian synchronized swimmers came a graceful second to the Americans in the new synchro team event.

All of these placings, as the Games moved deeper into their second week, fed Canadians' expectations. They wanted more, and the athletes delivered, athletes in many sports and in many combinations.

Team sports? The eight young women of the synchronized swimming team—a group that included Barcelona gold medallist Sylvie Fréchette—swam sublimely and won silver in a contest where the American women's performance wrung a perfect 100 score from the judges in the free routine. Canada finished second with an overall total that left them slightly more than one point behind the Americans.

In the most grittily individual of the combat sports, boxing and wrestling, two new Canadians won dazzling silvers. Guivi Sissaouri, a young man who travelled from his home in the Republic of Georgia to Montreal in 1991 to train further as a wrestler, grappled for his silver in the 57-kilogram division in freestyle wrestling.

David Defiagbon, a boxer who emigrated from Nigeria and settled in Halifax, gave his all for his adopted country. His wins in the heavyweight division included one extraordinary episode. Defiagbon held a narrow 10-9 lead on points over France's Christophe Mendy with 2:03 to go in the third round of a preliminary bout when Defiagbon dropped to the canvas as if he had been axed. As he writhed on the floor of the ring, Defiagbon complained that Mendy had punched him low, right in the groin. Mendy called Defiagbon a fake. There had been no low blow, the Frenchman insisted. The judges dithered but finally came down on the Canadian boxer's side. Mendy was disqualified, and Defiagbon eventually moved to the final against Cuba's Felix Savon, who soundly trounced him 20-2. That was no disgrace. Savon, the defending Olympic champion, was probably the world's best amateur boxer. Defiagbon could be proud of his silver.

As could Montreal's Annie Pelletier of her bronze in the springboard diving event; young Clara Hughes of yet another bronze, this time in the individual time trial cycling race; and Caroline Brunet of her silver in the women's 500-metre kayak singles. The medals were piling up for Canada, just as Canadians had expected, but there was one lack. We were short of medals at the high end, in the golds.

Donovan Bailey and friends handled that deficiency with style and grace. Bailey of Oakville, Ontario, had captured the gold in the 100 metres, a scintillating race, at the midpoint of the Games. And now, with one day left in the Centennial Olympics, Bailey and his teammates lined up for the 4 × 100-metre relay: Robert Esmie of Sudbury (the one with his hair shaved to read "relay blast off"), Ottawa's Glenroy Gilbert, and Bruny Surin of Montreal. They were up against the strutting Americans, defending Olympic champions, part of a tradition that had never seen the United States defeated in this relay race, except by disqualification, in 84 years. The streak was about to end.

Robert Esmie, Canada's lead-off runner, followed the message on his scalp. He blasted off, and over the

Mark Heese (opposite) and John Child were ranked fifth in the world before they took the bronze medal in the new Olympic sport of beach volleyball.

first 100 metres he was within a hair of being even with the second-place American. Esmie handed off to Glenroy Gilbert, who streaked his in a dazzling 9.02 seconds. That pace opened up room between the Canadians and the Americans. Surin, Canada's next runner, was the master of the bend in the track on the third lap, and by the time he handed the baton to Bailey for the last lap, the race was just about in the bag. Bailey ran his 100 metres in 8.95 seconds. It might have been faster, but so far out in front was Bailey, so convinced of victory, that, with 15 metres left to run, he slowed and raised his hand in triumph. The Canadians' time was 0:37.69. The world record was 0:37.40. Except for Bailey's raised arm, the Canadians might have broken the record.

But who cared? Canada won. Canada beat the Americans. Canada won the gold. And the store of medals mounted. In the end it would be the largest medal haul for the country in any Olympics except for 1984, when the eastern bloc countries boycotted the Games. It was, in short, the best ever performance by a Canadian Olympic team.

Canadians hadn't expected anything less.

The Games' first-ever mountain bike event provided the opportunity for Vancouver's Alison Sydor (no. 3) to pedal to a silver medal in the two-hour off-road race.

Three cyclists, three medals: (clockwise) Curt Harnett hinted at retirement from international competition after his third Olympic medal win in Atlanta; Alison Sydor went to the Games with two world championships to her credit; Brian Walton cycled the points race of his career for his first Olympic medal.

Profile

Donovan Bailey

GOLD MEDALLIST, 100 M SPRINT AND 4 X 100 RELAY, 1996

For Canada, the moment of the 1996 Summer Games when most eyes watered up in patriotism came when Donovan Bailey accepted the huge Canadian flag from the white-haired lady in the front row at Olympic Stadium, wrapped himself in the red and white folds, and jogged his enormously stirring victory lap around the track.

That came moments after Bailey had crossed the finish line in the 100-metre dash in first place, in world record time. And *that* came many, many moments after the eight runners, arguably the fastest field ever to line up for the event in the history of track, first took their positions in the starting blocks. The runners were ready. Or were they?

First—in what became a dramatic, possibly shameful, certainly protracted series of episodes leading up to the real beginning—England's Linford Christie broke out in a false start. Then Ato Boldon of Trinidad did the same thing. Then Christie, against all common sense, repeated his blunder. Two false starts for Christie. He was disqualified from the race. But Christie, the defending Olympic champion at the distance, refused to go quietly. He stalled and gestured in anger at the officials. Did the delay unsettle the other runners? American sprinter Dennis Mitchell later called the race "the most unprofessional I've ever run in in my life." Donovan Bailey, blithe man, confident man, said, oh, well, the delay actually helped to relax him.

When, on the fourth try at a legitimate start, the runners burst from the blocks, Bailey came out in the slightly muffled break that identifies his races. He's never quick off the mark, and he wasn't on this night of all nights. But at 40 metres, he began to pick off the field. Twenty metres later, in much less time than it takes to read the words in this sentence, he became the man in charge.

Bailey powered down his lane so encased in raw acceleration that he seemed for an instant to be all alone in the race, this guy in the clean white jersey, "Canada" across his chest in red letters, number 1192, just so undeniably fast that at 80 metres he passed Ato Boldon (third place) and Namibia's Frankie Fredericks (second place) as if they were men who had happened into the wrong race. Bailey covered the 100 metres in 9.84 seconds, .01 seconds faster than Leroy Burrell's June 7, 1994, world record. Bailey won cleanly—no positives turned up in *his* post-race drug tests—and he won indisputably.

He was a man Canada could hail, a man of intelligence, integrity and, accomplishment away from the track. This last was probably crucial to his success in sprinting. Before he became serious about running, when he was still barely out of his teens, he graduated from Sheridan

With his victories in the 100 m and the 4 x 100 m relay in Atlanta, Donovan Bailey became the first Canadian track athlete to bring home two gold medals from a single Summer Games since Percy Williams in 1928.

208

College near his home town of Oakville with a diploma in economics and parlayed it into a business career. He made money with a line of clothing, in the import-export game, in real estate, with some investment dabbling. At 22, he owned a house and a Porsche, and when at last he concentrated on track, it was with the knowledge that running wouldn't define his life. No wonder he was blithe and confident, cooler than the other competitors, during the delay in the race that brought him—and Canada—the gold in Atlanta.

So what if he later billed himself as a hyphenated Canadian, a Jamaican-Canadian. He was entitled; he spent his first 12 years in Jamaica, and his mother, the largest influence on his life, still lived on the island. Hyphenated Canadian, okay, but whose flag did Bailey wrap himself in at the end of the greatest race of any sprinter's life? Canada's beloved Maple Leaf never looked better.

Pundits estimated that Bailey's Atlanta wins would earn him between $4 and $5 million a year in endorsements.

The gold medal-winning 4 x 100 relay team of Bruny Surin, Glenroy Gilbert, Donovan Bailey, and Robert Esmie served notice to the Americans that their 84-year domination of the event was over.

THE 1996 CANADIAN OLYMPIC TEAM

ARCHERY
Jennot Robitaille
Rob Rusnov
Kevin Sally

ATHLETICS
May Allison
Katie Anderson
Ladonna Antoine
Donovan Bailey
Danuta Bartoszek
Tim Berrett
Catherine Bond-Mills
Joel Bourgeois
Kathy Butler
Carlton Chambers
Charmaine Crooks
Bruce Deacon
Nicole Devonish
Richard Duncan
Rosey Edeh
Robert Esmie
Peter Fonseca
O'Brian Gibbons
Glenroy Gilbert
Graham Hood
Arturo Huerta
Tim Kroeker
Charles Lefrançois
Janice McCaffrey
Robyn Meagher
Carey Nelson
Peter Ogilvie
Sonia Paquette
Leah Pells
Tarama Perry

Tina Poitras
Jeffrey Schiebler
Paula Schnurr
Michael Smith
Brad Snyder
Martin St. Pierre
Kevin Sullivan
Bruny Surin
Lesley Tashlin
Jason Tunks

Wheelchair
Chantal Petitclerc

BADMINTON
Jaimie Dawson
Si-an Deng
Denyse Julien
Anil Kaul
Doris Piché
Iain Sydie
Darryl Yung

BASKETBALL
Andrea Blackwell
Kelly Boucher
Jodi Evans
Martina Jerant
Cynthia Johnston
Karla Karch-Gailus
Merlelynn Lange-Harris
Shawna Molcak
Dianne Norman
Beverly Smith
Sue Stewart
Camille Thompson

BOXING
Jean François Bergeron
Phil Boudreault
David Defiagbon
Nick Farrell
Dominic Figliomeni
Hercules Kyvelos
Claude Lambert
Casey Patton
Troy Amos Ross
Mike Strange
Randall Thompson

CANOE/KAYAK
Mihai Apostal
Sheryl Boyle
Caroline Brunet
Tamas Buday
Atilla Buday
Renn Critchlow
David Ford
Benoît Gauthier
Eric Gervais
Marie Josée Gibeau
Peter Giles
Steve Giles
Allison Herst
Dan Howe
Liam Jewell
Corrina Kennedy
Margaret Langford
François Letourneau
Klari MacAskill
Gavin Maxwell
Larry Norman
Kelly O'Leary

CYCLING

Michael Barry

Steve Bauer

Tanya Dubnicoff

Gord Fraser

Curt Harnett

Andreas Hestler

Clara Hughes

Linda Jackson

Jacques Landry

Sue Palmer

Warren Sallenback

Alison Sydor

Lesley Tomlinson

Brian Walton

Eric Wohlberg

DIVING

David Bedard

Eryn Bulmer

Philippe Comtois

Paige Gordon

Anne Montminy

Annie Pelletier

EQUESTRIAN

Leonie Bramall

Mac Cone

Christopher Delia

Tom Dvorak

Chelan Kozak

Ian Millar

Kelli McMullen-Temple

Claire Smith

Gina Smith

Linda Southern

Evi Strasser

Therese Washtock

Stuart Young-Black

FENCING

Jean-Marie Banos

Jean-Paul Banos

Jean-Marc Chouinard

Evans Gravel

Dan Nowosielski

Tony Plourde

James Ransom

GYMNASTICS–ARTISTIC

Kris Burley

Jennifer Exaltacion

Richard Ikeda

Shanyn MacEachern

Alan Nolet

Yvonne Tousek

GYMNASTICS–RHYTHMIC

Camille Martens

JUDO

Ewan Beaton

Michelle Buckingham

Nancy Filteau

Nicolas Gill

Natalie Gosselin

Niki Jenkins

Carolyne Lepage

Keith Morgan

Colin Morgan

Marie-Josée Morneau

Taro Tan

ROWING

Darren Barber

Laryssa Biesenthal

David Boyes

Scott Brodie

Andrew Crosby

Michael Forgeron

Phil Graham

Todd Hallett

Gavin Hassett

Kathleen Heddle

Henry Hering

Alison Korn

Silken Laumann

Jeffrey Lay

Theresa Luke

Maria Maunder

Marnie McBean

Heather McDermid

Colleen Miller

Jessica Monroe

Patrick Newman

Diane O'Grady

Adam Parfitt

Brian Peaker

Mark Platt

Derek Porter

Emma Robinson

Greg Stevenson

Lesley Thompson

Tosha Tsang

Anna van der Kamp

Wendy Wiebe

SHOOTING

Rod Boll

Jason Caswell

Michel Dion

George Leary

Cynthia Meyer

Clayton Miller

Kirk Reynolds

Jean-François Senécal

Paul Shaw

SOFTBALL

Sandra Beasley

Juanita Clayton

Karen Doell

Carrie Flemmer

Kelly Kelland

Pauline Maurice

Kara McGaw

Candace Murray

Christine Parris-Washington

Lori Sippel

Karen Snelgrove
Deb Sonnenberg
Alecia Stephenson
Colleen Thorburn
Carmie Vairo

SWIMMING
Jessica Amey
Casey Barrett
Rob Braknis
Stephen Clarke
Jon Cleveland
Guylaine Cloutier
Jessica Deglau
Martina Dessureault
Nikki Dryden
Sarah Evanetz
Lisa Flood
Julie Howard
Hugues Legault
Marianne Limpert
Joanne Malar
Riley Mants
Andrea Moody
Curtis Myden
Laura Nicholls
Eddie Parenti
Christin Petelski
Chris Renaud
Stephanie Richardson
Andrea Schwartz
Shannon Shakespeare
Sophie Simard
Nancy Sweetnam

SYNCHRONIZED SWIMMING
Lisa Alexander
Janice Bremner
Karen Clark
Karen Fonteyne
Sylvie Fréchette
Valerie Hould-Marchand
Kasia Kulesza

Christine Larsen
Cari Read
Erin Woodley

TABLE TENNIS
Petra Cada
Barbara Chiu
Lijuan Geng
Johnny Huang
Gideon Joe Ng

TENNIS
Grant Connell
Jill Hetherington
Patricia Hy-Boulais
Sebastien Lareau
Jana Nejedly
Daniel Nestor

VOLLEYBALL
Barb Broen-Ouelette
Kerri Ann Buchberger
John Child
Josée Corbeil
Ed Drakich
Marc Dunn
Wanda Guenette
Mark Heese
Janis Kelly
Margo Malowney
Lori Ann Mundt
Diane Ratnik
Erminia Russo
Michelle Sawatzky
Brigitte Soucy
Christine Stark
Kathryn Tough
Katrina von Sass

WEIGHTLIFTING
Jean Lavertue
Serge Tremblay

WRESTLING
Colbie Bell
Scott Bianco
Andrew Borodow
Marty Calder
Doug Cox
Colin Daynes
David Hohl
Yogi Johl
Oleg Ladik
Paul Ragusa
Craig Roberts
Ainsley Robinson
Guivi Sissaouri
Greg Woodcroft

YACHTING
Bill Abbott
Joanne Abbott
Caroll-Ann Alie
Leigh Andrew-Pearson
Alain Bolduc
Brad Boston
Richard Clarke
Rod Davies
Penny (Stamper) Davis
Paul Hannam
Roy Janse
Eric Jespersen
Ross MacDonald
Tine Moberg-Parker
Marc Peers
Brian Storey

LIST OF CONTRIBUTORS

JAMES A. BARCLAY is a respected writer on sports and the author of *Golf in Canada: A History*.

BRAD BATTEN is a published poet and a journalist.

JACK BATTEN is the author of 29 books, including several bestsellers on the Canadian legal scene, and six titles about sports ranging from jogging and skiing, through to hockey and basketball.

FRANK COSENTINO, a former CFL quarterback, intercollegiate football coach, and current professor of Physical Education and Athletics at York University, has written numerous books about Canadian sports history, including two previous titles on the Olympics.

JOE COTÉ is a popular Toronto broadcaster, host of CBC Radio's "Ontario Morning," and a journalist who has written widely on sports and travel for Canadian and American newspapers.

DEREK FINKLE has published features in *Saturday Night*, *Toronto Life*, and the *Globe and Mail*.

TRENT FRAYNE is one of Canada's foremost sportswriters. In addition to a distinguished career in journalism, he has published several acclaimed books, including *Tales of an Athletic Supporter* and *The Best of Times: Fifty Years of Canadian Sport*.

WILLIAM HUMBER is the chair of the Faculty of Continuing Education at Seneca College in Toronto. He is the author of eight books, including *All I Thought About Was Baseball: Writings on a Canadian Pastime*, *Diamonds of the North: A Concise History of Baseball in Canada*, and two children's titles on baseball and soccer.

DOUGLAS HUNTER has written four books, including *A Breed Apart: An Illustrated History of Goaltending* and *Open Ice: The Tim Horton Story*. He has also been a staff writer with the *Financial Post* and editor of *Canadian Yachting*.

STEVEN MILTON is the author of *Skate!: 100 Years of Figure Skating*, *Super Skaters: World Figure Skating Stars*, and *Orser: A Skater's Life*.

KAREN O'REILLY has written *Running Risks*, a biography of runner Angella Issajenko, and numerous articles for a wide variety of newspapers and magazines.

CAROL PHILLIPS is an award-winning writer whose background includes magazine, newspaper, and wire service journalism. She is currently a reporter with the *Hamilton Spectator*.

INDEX

PHOTO CREDITS

Photographs are credited clockwise from top left of the page where they appear.

THE FOLLOWING ABBREVIATIONS ARE USED: COA, Canadian Olympic Association; **CP**, Canapress; **CSHF**, Canada's Sports Hall of Fame; **CSI**, Canadian Sports Images; principal photographers F. Scott Grant, Ted Grant, Claus Andersen, Mike Ridewood; **CW**, Canada Wide/Toronto Sun; **HHF**, The Hockey Hall of Fame; **JBC**, James Barclay Collection; **JWC**, James Worrall Collection; **NA**, National Archives of Canada; **OM**, Olympic Museum, Lausanne, Switzerland; **SO**, Swim Ontario; **TS**, Toronto Star; **WHC**, William Humber Collection.

COVER: WHC, CSI (C. Andersen)

CHAPTER ONE: p8, JBC, OM; p9, CSHF; p10, COA, COA; p11, COA; p12, Notman/CSHF; p13, WHC, CSHF, CSHF; p14, OM; p15, CSHF; p16, NA #PA28957, CSHF; p18, CSHF, WHC; p19, CSHF; p20, COA; p21, CSHF; p22, CSHF, CSHF; p23, COA; p24, CSHF; p25, CSHF.

CHAPTER TWO: p26, CSHF, CSI; p27, NA #PA15099; p28, CSHF; p29, OM; p30, COA; p31, CSHF; p32, CSHF; p33 OM; p34, HHF; p36, HHF; p37, NA #PA151001; p38, CSHF; p39, NA #PA150994; p40, CSHF; p41, COA, NA #PA150992; p42, CSHF; p43, WHC; p45, WHC.

CHAPTER THREE: p46, OM; p47, OM; p48, CSHF, COA; p49, CSHF; p50, COA; p51, CSHF; p52, SO; p53, WHC, CSHF; p54, WHC; p55, CSHF, COA; p56, COA; p58, OM; p59, OM; p60, JWC; p61, OM; p62, OM; p63, COA; p64, CSHF; p65 COA; p66, COA.

CHAPTER FOUR: p68, CSHF, OM; p69, CSHF; p71, CSHF; p72, HHF; p73, OM; p75, CSHF; p76, CSHF; p77, CSHF; p78, OM; p79, CSHF; p80, OM; p81, COA; p82, CSHF; p84, CSHF; p85, NA #C25364.

CHAPTER FIVE: p86, CSHF; COA 72S-CE-218; p87, COA; p88, CP; p89, COA 72S-X5W-16; p90, NA #K68-0047-48; p91, COA 68W-NT-1; p92, NA #K72-00497-31; p93, NA #K72-00497-24; p95, NA #K68-00032-8; p96, COA; p97, OM; p98, NA #PA127391; p99, NA #CK72-01664-3; p100, COA 72-NT-61, COA 72S-XAT-710; p101, COA 72S-CE-77, p102 CSHF.

CHAPTER SIX: p104, COA 76S-XEQ-484, COA 76S-CE-868; p105, NA #K76-00390-7; p106, COA 76W-GM-42; p107, NA #K76-00111-12; p108, NA #K76-00104-90, NA #PA145063; p109, NA #K76-00390-12; p110, COA 76S-OS-544; p111, COA 76-OS-0299, OM; p112, NA #K76-00412-76; p113, NA #K76-00412-3, COA 76S XEQ-532; p114, COA; p115, COA 76S-SP-115; p117, COA 76W-ML-18.

CHAPTER SEVEN: All photos from CSI except: p118, Norm Betts/CW (right); p123, OM; p125, COA 84W-ML-25 (left); p133, COA 84S-ML-28.

CHAPTER EIGHT: All photos from CSI except: p138, NA # PA175370, NA #38, p139 NA #8.

CHAPTER NINE: All photos from CSI.

CHAPTER TEN: All photos from CSI.

CHAPTER ELEVEN: p190, CSI; p191, CSI, CSI; p192, CSI; p193, CSI; p194, CW; p195, Bernard Weil/TS; p196, CSI; p197, CSI; p198, Peter Power/TS, Peter Power/TS; p199, CSI; p200, CSI; p201, Peter Power/TS; p202, CSI, Peter Power/TS; p203, Bernard Weil/TS; p204, Bernard Weil/TS, CSI; p205, CSI; p206, CSI; p207, CSI, CSI, CSI; p209, CSI; p210, CSI; p211, CSI; p212, CSI.

SPECIAL THANKS TO: Canadian Olympic Association's Sylvia Doucette; Allan Stewart & Debbie Chevarie at Canada's Sport Hall of Fame; the staff at the National Archives; Craig Campbell at Hockey Hall of Fame; Debbie Prince at Swim Ontario; Catherine Chapuis at Olympic Museum, Lausanne; Pedda Jungmann, photo research assistant. A medal goes to Sandy Grant at Canadian Sport Images for her organization and speed in meeting our deadlines.